FREEDOM VS. INTERVENTION

FREEDOM VS. INTERVENTION

Six Tough Cases

Daniel E. Lee

ROWMAN & LITTLEFIELD PUBLISHERS, INC.
Lanham • Boulder • New York • Toronto • Oxford

ROWMAN & LITTLEFIELD PUBLISHERS, INC.

Published in the United States of America
by Rowman & Littlefield Publishers, Inc.
A wholly owned subsidiary of The Rowman & Littlefield Publishing Group, Inc.
4501 Forbes Boulevard, Suite 200, Lanham, Maryland 20706
www.rowmanlittlefield.com

PO Box 317
Oxford
OX2 9RU, UK

British Library Cataloguing in Publication Information Available

Library of Congress Cataloging-in-Publication Data

Lee, Daniel E.
 Freedom vs. intervention : six tough cases / Daniel E. Lee.
   p. cm.
 Includes bibliographical references and index.
 ISBN 0-7425-4210-6 (cloth : alk. paper) — ISBN 0-7425-4211-4 (pbk. : alk.
paper)
 1. Law—Moral and ethical aspects—United States. 2. Public policy
(Law)—United States. 3. United States—Social policy. 4. Political questions
and judicial power—United States. I. Title. KF384.L44 2005
 342.7308—dc22
                                   2004025144

Printed in the United States of America

♾™ The paper used in this publication meets the minimum requirements of
American National Standard for Information Sciences—Permanence of Paper
for Printed Library Materials, ANSI/NISO Z39.48–1992.

CONTENTS

—

PREFACE

—

In a sense, this volume is a sequel to *Navigating Right and Wrong* (2002), in which I argue that there is no place on which we can stand and judge the whole world. Rather than succumb to the vanity of "mountain top morality," I suggest that we should opt for "ethics on the horizontal" in the valley below by being open and responsive to the humanity of those whose lives intersect with ours. In deciding what is right or wrong, we can do no more than acknowledge that the value claims we make are part of the faiths we affirm—faiths that can be religious or entirely secular in nature. And in talking about our obligations, all we can do is make reference to the values we affirm; it is these affirmations of faith that bind us in conscience.

All of this, however, leaves an important question hanging: when, if at all, is it appropriate for us to intervene in the lives of other people? If the best that we can do is to refer to the values that bind us in conscience, does this by implication mean that we should in all cases stand aside and let others do whatever they might be inclined to do? Hardly. As Martin Luther King Jr. and others have recognized, there are times that the faith to which one is committed compels action. And when it comes to using the legal system as a tool for intervention, there is broad public support for laws prohibiting murder, sexual assault, child abuse, and other injurious acts.

These, however, are the easy cases. When it comes to matters such as motorcycle helmets, physician-assisted suicide, and abortion, questions of intervention elicit sharply differing responses. Since hard cases are far more interesting—intellectually and practically—than those about which there is little disagreement, this volume is devoted to discussion of these types of cases.

I do not expect everyone to agree with the positions that I take—or for that matter, that anyone will agree with the positions taken on all of these controversial issues. But of respectful disagreement, moral discourse is made. Such discourse is possible only if views and perspectives are presented in a straightforward, thoughtful manner. So doing is what this volume is intended to help accomplish.

I began this volume while on sabbatical during spring term of the 2001–2002 academic year. I am appreciative of Augustana College for providing sabbatical support. I am indebted to Steven C. Bahls, Elizabeth J. Lee, Kristy Nabhan-Warren, and James M. Rettig for reading various portions of the manuscript and making numerous helpful suggestions. Comments by the two anonymous readers who reviewed the manuscript for the publisher were similarly helpful. It was a delight to work with Eve DeVaro Fowler, editor for philosophy at Rowman & Littlefield Publishers, Inc.; her assistant, Tessa Fallon; Lynn Weber, the production editor for this book; and Scott Jerard, who did the line editing. Any remaining errors, of course, are solely my responsibility and should in no way be blamed on those who were kind enough to read the manuscript and share with me their thoughts and suggestions.

INTRODUCTION

—

When, if at all, is it appropriate to intervene in the lives of other people, either to prevent them from doing something we do not think they should be doing or to force them to do something we think they should do? Is everyone's business our business? Or is intervening in the lives of others unwarranted intrusion?

Issues related to intervention are particularly complicated when they involve questions of public policy. When the government intervenes, the coercive power of the legal system, complete with threats of imprisonment or heavy fines, can be brought to bear on those who contemplate violating the law. When, if ever, is a government justified in intervening in the lives of private citizens, either to prevent them from acting in ways viewed as inappropriate or to force them to do whatever is viewed as desirable?[1]

Coercive intervention by its very nature is costly. Putting together and maintaining regulatory and law enforcement agencies costs money—a lot of money. In a report issued in 2003, the federal government's Office of Management and Budget estimated the cost of major federal regulations to be somewhere between $38 billion and $44 billion each year.[2] In fiscal 2001 (the most recent year for which comprehensive statistics are available), the total amount federal, state, and local governments spent for police protection, corrections, and judicial and legal activities was more than $167 billion—approximately $600 for each man, woman, and child in this country.[3]

Coercive intervention is also costly in terms of individual liberty, for it prevents people from doing what they want to do and forces them to do what they don't want to do. Granted, acts of intervention are not equally costly. Utilizing the doctrine of eminent domain to force the sale of private property so that a new highway can be built is far more costly in terms of individual liberty than are forms of intervention that merely inconvenience people—for example, laws prohibiting parking in loading zones. Yet, though the magnitude of the cost varies, a common feature of all forms of coercive intervention is that they always impose costs on those subjected to coercion (and, in various ways and to varying degrees, often on others as well).

Because of the costs, intervention in the lives of others is at best the lesser of evils. This element of reluctance roughly parallels that reflected in traditional just war theory, which, though originally formulated to provide guidelines for military intervention, provides useful reference points for discussing domestic public policy questions. The reluctance that characterizes just war theory is brought into clear focus by a well-known typology that the widely read church historian Roland Bainton (1894–1984) developed in *Christian Attitudes toward War and Peace*. Bainton identifies three perspectives toward lethal violence that can be found in Christian thought: the crusade, the just war, and pacifism. The crusade, which Bainton also labels "the holy war," reflects a very positive and at times even enthusiastic view of war that promotes a cause to which one is dedicated. Pacifism, Bainton's own view, completely rejects lethal violence. Just war theory is somewhere in between. As do pacifists, just war theorists view all loss of human life as deeply regrettable, indeed tragic. However, as do those who take a crusading approach, just war theorists believe that the cause of justice sometimes compels action. The combination of these countervailing tendencies results in the reluctance that characterizes just war theory.[4]

Both with respect to questions of military intervention (which are not addressed in this volume) and public policy involving coercive intervention (several of which are addressed in this volume), the balanced and reluctant approach reflected in just war theory has always struck me as having much to recommend it. Intervening anytime anyone else is doing anything that we believe is inappropriate can create more problems than it solves, all the while significantly undermining individual liberty. However, taking a completely *laissez-faire* approach—to remain completely disengaged regardless of what others might be doing—risks allowing grave harm to occur in situations in which the actions of some threaten the lives, health, and well-being of others. The middle approach provides appropriate balance: it allows intervention in some situations but not all, and it characterizes the intervention as the lesser of evils and as the decision made with at least some degree of reluctance.

But if intervention is allowed in some situations but not others, what counts as a justifiable reason for intervention? When what some might do poses a significant risk to the lives, health, and well-being of others, a strong case can be made for intervention to protect those who are threatened. It is for this reason that laws prohibiting murder, sexual assault, child abuse, and other acts injurious to others receive broad public support, and appropriately so. The case for intervention is far more difficult to make, however, when the consequences of the act are borne primarily by the perpetrator of the act, as is the case with physician-assisted suicide, riding a motorcycle without a helmet, and many other matters of controversy. Is our not liking what others might be inclined to do (or not do) a sufficient reason for intervention?

In a society that places strong emphasis on the freedom of the individual, it is difficult to defend intervening in the lives of others simply because we do not like what they are doing or because we believe that they ought to be doing something they are not inclined to do. In *On*

Liberty, John Stuart Mill (1806–1873) cautions, "A person should be free to do as he likes in his own concerns, but he ought not be free to do as he likes in acting for another, under the pretext that the affairs of the other are his own affairs."[5] The claim "I know what is best for you" or "Government knows best" is a strong one indeed—one that flies in the face of the most basic notions of liberty. In situations in which others are capable of making their own decisions, we have neither the right nor the wisdom to make their decisions for them.

But like many other matters, closer examination uncovers greater complexity. A distinction is often made between *soft (weak) paternalism*—intervening to secure an outcome consistent with the values held by those who are being coerced—and *hard (strong) paternalism*—intervening because those doing the intervening believe they know what is best for others.[6] The case for soft paternalism is much stronger than the case for hard paternalism.[7] Because of deficiencies in our decision-making processes or because of failures of our will, we sometimes act in ways at odds with our own deeply held values and desires. In such cases, coercive intervention, distasteful though it might be, can have the salutary effect of forcing us to do what we in fact really want to do. Mill provides the following example:

> If either a public officer or anyone else saw a person attempting to cross a bridge which had been ascertained to be unsafe, and there was not time to warn him of his danger, they might seize him and turn him back, without any real infringement of his liberty; for liberty consists in doing what one desires, and he does not desire to fall into the river.[8]

In a thoughtful little book published three decades ago, social philosopher Joel Feinberg suggests that the degree of voluntariness is the key factor in determining the extent to which intervention is in order.[9] And indeed, Mill would agree that intervention is in order if the person in question is "a child, or delirious, or in some state of excitement or absorption incompatible with the full use of the reflecting faculty."[10] Commenting on this passage from *On Liberty*, Feinberg observes, "Nevertheless, there are some actions that create a powerful presumption that an actor in his right mind would not choose them." The stronger the presumption, "the more elaborate and fastidious should be the legal paraphernalia required, and the stricter the standards of evidence" if that presumption is to be overridden. He concludes, "The point of the procedure would not be to evaluate the wisdom or worthiness of a person's choice, but rather to determine whether the choice really is his."[11]

We will return to these matters when addressing particular issues of intervention, such as laws requiring motorcyclists to wear helmets and the question of whether physician-assisted suicide should be legalized. Some other preliminary matters, however, remain to be discussed. Traditional just war theorists have always insisted that having a just cause, while a necessary condition, is not a sufficient reason to justify intervention. Other criteria must also be satisfied, among them right intent, last resort, lawful authority, reasonable hope of success, and due proportionality.[12]

In specifying right intent, just war theorists insist that intervention must be done for the right reasons—for example, defending those who are threatened—and not just to stir up trouble or relieve boredom. As for last resort, because intervention is unpleasant business that interferes significantly with the freedom of the individual, a strong case can be made for insisting that intervention is appropriate only when all else has failed. As just war theory holds that diplomatic efforts to resolve international controversy should be exhausted before military action is taken,[13] so also should other ways of changing the behavior or resolving the problem be exhausted before resorting to coercive intervention. The behavioral patterns of others can sometimes be changed by informing them of the risks inherent in what they are doing, by engaging in gentle persuasion, or by offering financial incentives (such as lower insurance rates for nonsmokers). If behavioral patterns can be changed by measures such as these, there is not a case to be made for coercive intervention. And in cases such as Jehovah's Witnesses who refuse to allow blood transfusions, sometimes there are alternate forms of therapy available, in which case coercive intervention would not satisfy the criterion of last resort.

Throughout the centuries, just war theorists have insisted that military action be conducted under the auspices of lawful authority. Augustine (354–430) suggested that for a war to be just, "a great deal depends" on the authority that those waging war "have for doing so."[14] The first condition that Thomas Aquinas (1224/1225–1274) specifies, in mapping out the conditions that must be satisfied if a war is to be just, is that war must be waged under the authority of a sovereign, "for it is not the business of a private person to declare war."[15] Augustine, Aquinas, and the other just war theorists who place strong emphasis on lawful authority do so for an important reason: acts of violence perpetrated by private individuals are more difficult to control and are less likely to be restrained.[16]

What is true of intervention in the affairs of other nations is true of domestic intervention as well. While there might be some instances in which intervention by private individuals is appropriate—for example, intervening to ward off an assailant when no police officers are in the vicinity—there is much to be said for orderly processes of intervention via official channels with appropriate emphasis on due process. Vigilante action and other private acts of intervention risk destructive chaos rather than resolution of the problem.

The criteria for reasonable hope of success and due proportionality serve to remind us that we ought not do something just for the sake of doing something. If coercive intervention is to be justified, it must on balance make the situation better rather than worse. To have any prospect of improving the situation, it must succeed, of course. Since, as already noted, intervention by its very nature is always costly, futile efforts to intervene invariably make the situation worse and are hence inappropriate. Granted, since the future by definition is difficult to study, we never know for certain how things will turn out. However, it is usually possible to make some type of assessment about what the probabilities of success are. Military planners, for example, know that missions without appropriate logistical support are likely to fail and are hence ill-considered, even if initiated to address a grievous wrong. The same is true of most other forms of intervention.

The notion of due proportionality reminds us that success alone is not enough. Because intervention is always costly, whatever is gained by winning must be sufficient to offset the cost of victory. Many historical examples can be cited of wars in which both sides ended up losing more than they gained even though one side was nominally the victor. The Crimean War (1854–1856) and the Russo-Japanese War (1904–1905) are but two examples of many such tragedies.

The same is true of government intervention in the lives of its citizens. A classic textbook example of intervention gone awry is prohibition. Today, we often forget that the prohibition movement was motivated in substantial measure by sincere concerns about the human cost of alcohol abuse—families left destitute when the primary wage earner lost his or her job because of alcohol abuse, alcohol-related marital problems, and many other costs both personal and social. As all students of American history are keenly aware, the attempted solution— prohibition of the sale and consumption of alcoholic beverages— created a whole new set of problems, among them disrespect for law and a fertile environment for organized crime. The historical experience of prohibition serves to remind us that doing something just because we think that we ought to be doing something can result in more harm than good.

And so, when addressing questions of intervention, we have a lot to consider—a complex variety of factors that we need to take into account. This is not to suggest that all questions of intervention are complicated matters. Just about everyone would agree that intervention to prevent child abuse is warranted (though there are differences of opinion about matters such as how much evidence of abuse is needed before intervention is in order). And no one today argues that efforts should be made to reinstate the Connecticut law struck down by the U.S. Supreme Court in the *Griswold* decision in 1965, a law that prohibited married couples from using contraceptives.[17] There is broad consensus today that what people do in the privacy of their bedrooms is not the business of the government and that attempts to regulate private sexual practices are highly inappropriate.

These, however, are the easy cases. Far more difficult are matters about which there is no consensus, such as laws regarding motorcycle helmets, physician-assisted suicide, recreational marijuana use, abortion, parental refusal to allow children to receive blood transfusions or other beneficial medical treatment, and environmental regulations that place limits on what property owners can do with their property. To these matters we now turn.

NOTES

1. Not all forms of government intervention, it should be noted, are coercive. For example, a government might subject citizens to endless propaganda advocating certain courses of action without in any way threatening them with arrest and imprisonment if they fail to take these courses of action. Similarly, government intervention in the form of providing tax breaks and other economic incentives is noncoercive if those who choose to forego the benefits offered by these incentives face no threat of legal action and do not risk finding themselves in desperate circumstances, financial or otherwise.

2. Office of Management and Budget, *Draft 2003 Report to Congress on the Costs and Benefits of Federal Regulations,* at http://usgovinfo.about.com/gi/dynamic/offsite.htm?site=http://www.whitehouse.gov/omb/fedreg/2003draft%5Fcost%2Dbenefit%5Frpt.pdf (accessed August 22, 2004). The report estimates that these regulations provide between $135 billion and $218 billion of benefits to taxpayers each year.

3. United States Department of Justice, Bureau of Justice Statistics, *Expenditure and Employment Statistics,* at www.ojp.usdoj.gov/bjs/eande.htm (accessed August 22, 2004).

4. Roland Bainton, *Christian Attitudes toward War and Peace: A Historical Survey and Critical Re-evaluation* (Nashville, Tenn.: Abingdon Press, 1960), 14, 242–51.

5. John Stuart Mill, *On Liberty,* ed. Currin V. Shields (Indianapolis, Ind.: Bobbs-Merrill, 1956), 127.

6. See, for example, Tom L. Beauchamp and James F. Childress, *Principles of Biomedical Ethics,* 4th ed. (New York: Oxford University Press, 1994), 277–78.

7. Beauchamp and Childress make a narrowly defined case for strong paternalism in a very limited set of circumstances. They write, "Although strong paternalism is a dangerous position that is subject to abuse, conditions can be specified that restrict the range of interventions and that justify only a narrow range of acts. In reaching this conclusion, we do not defend public and institutional *policies* of strong paternalism, but only certain *acts* of strong paternalism." The examples they cite involve situations in which physicians believe that withholding information from a particular patient or refusing to comply with the patient's wishes with respect to minor matters (e.g., having the side rails on the hospital bed up) is in the patient's best interests. However, the authors soften even these examples by adding that they "are tempted to add . . . a condition requiring that the paternalistic action not substantially restrict autonomy" (*Principles of Biomedical Ethics,* 382–83).

8. Mill, *On Liberty,* 117.

9. Joel Feinberg, *Social Philosophy* (Englewood Cliffs, N.J.: Prentice Hall, 1973), 48–52.

10. Mill, *On Liberty,* 117.

11. Feinberg, *Social Philosophy,* 49–51.

12. In *Contra Faustum,* Augustine states, with respect to the question of what constitutes a just war, "A great deal depends on the causes for which men undertake wars, and on the authority they have for doing so; for the natural order which seeks the peace of mankind, ordains that the monarch should have the power of undertaking war if he thinks it advisable, and that the soldiers should perform their military duties in behalf of the peace and safety of the community" (*Contra Faustum* 22.75, tr. Richard Stothert, in *A Select Library of the Nicene and Post-Nicene Fathers of The Christian Church,* vol. 4,

Writings in Connection with the Manichaean Controversy, ed. Philip Schaff [Grand Rapids, Mich.: Wm. B. Eerdmans Publishing, 1887], 301). In *Summa Theologica,* Thomas Aquinas suggests that three conditions must be met if a war is to be just: "First, the authority of the sovereign by whose command the war is to be waged. For it is not the business of a private person to declare war. . . . Second, a just cause is required, namely that those who are attacked should be attacked because they deserve it on account of some fault. . . . Third, it is necessary that the belligerents should have a right intention, so that they intend the advancement of good, or the avoidance of evil" (*Summa Theologica* 2.2, Q40, A1, tr. Fathers of the English Dominican Province, rev. Daniel J. Sullivan, Great Books of the Western World, vol. 20 [Chicago: Encyclopedia Britannica, 1952], 578). Hugo Grotius, while deemphasizing *jus ad bellum* (justice in going to war), and placing greater emphasis on *jus in bello* (justice in the conduct of war), insisted that war be conducted under the authority of a sovereign and that a declaration of war be issued: "It is essential to the nature of a public war that it should have the support of the sovereign power. . . . A declaration of war is also requisite" (*The Law of War and Peace [De Jure Belli ac Pacis Libri Tres]* 3.4–5, tr. Francis W. Kelsey [Indianapolis, Ind.: Bobbs-Merrill, 1925], 633). Summarizing classical just war theory, James Turner Johnson lists the major *jus ad bellum* criteria as just cause, right authority, right intent, proportionality, the end of peace, and last resort (*Can Modern War Be Just?* 18). James F. Childress lists the traditional *jus ad bellum* criteria as just cause, last resort, announcement of intentions, reasonable hope of success, proportionality, and just intention (James F. Childress, "Just-War Criteria," in *War or Peace? The Search for New Answers,* ed. Thomas A. Shannon [Maryknoll, N.Y.: Orbis Books, 1980], 46–48), while Ralph Potter adds highest lawful authority to the list (*War and Moral Discourse* [Richmond, Va.: John Knox Press, 1969], 43–44).

13. In popular contemporary thought about the ethics of international intervention, there is a certain tendency to rank various means of intervention as follows: diplomatic intervention, economic sanctions, military action, and assassination (if indeed assassination is on the list at all). In keeping with the notion of last resort, the implication is that those formulating foreign policy ought to go down the list only as far as is necessary to secure the desired outcome. The assumption is that each step down takes one further away from the moral high ground. Such a position is open to question. It is not a foregone conclusion that economic sanctions are "nicer" or more moral than military

action or that military action is preferable to political assassination. When economic sanctions cripple an aggressor nation's economy, the poor and the less privileged invariably bear the brunt of the costs. The ruling elite always have plenty to eat. Similarly, when aerial bombing and other forms of military action are used in an effort to get leaders of aggressor nations to change their ways, the bombs are more likely to kill innocent bystanders than rogue leaders hidden away in well-protected bomb shelters. While there is something very unsavory about attempting to assassinate rogue leaders, such efforts at least have the virtue of targeting the individuals most responsible for the atrocities they are perpetrating.

14. Augustine, *Contra Faustum* 22.75.

15. Aquinas, *Summa Theologica* 2.2, Q40, A1.

16. Given the strong emphasis on lawful authority that plays such a prominent role in the just war tradition, the question of whether revolution is ever justifiable has been a difficult one for just war theorists. One of the more interesting discussions of the morality of revolution is found in Reinhold Niebuhr's *Moral Man and Immoral Society* (New York: Charles Scribner's Sons), first published in 1932, at a time that Niebuhr was moving away from the pacifism he espoused in the wake of the horrific devastation of the First World War. In this widely read volume, Niebuhr states, "If a season of violence can establish a just social system and can create the possibilities of its preservation, there is no purely ethical ground upon which violence and revolution can be ruled out. . . . Once we have made the fateful concession of ethics to politics, and accepted coercion as a necessary instrument of social cohesion, we can make no absolute distinctions between non-violent and violent types of coercion or between coercion used by governments and that which is used by revolutionaries" (179).

17. *Griswold v. Connecticut*, 381 U.S. 479 (1965).

1

MOTORCYCLE HELMET LAWS

—

The facts about motorcycle helmets can be quite simply summarized: they save lives and reduce serious injury. Consider the following:

- The U.S. National Highway Traffic Safety Administration (NHTSA) reports that unhelmeted motorcyclists involved in crashes are 40 percent more likely to suffer a fatal head injury and 15 percent more likely to suffer a nonfatal injury than those who use helmets. Head injury is the leading cause of death for motorcyclists involved in crashes. The NHTSA estimates that from 1984 to 2002, helmets saved the lives of 13,774 motorcyclists and that, had all motorcyclists worn helmets during that period, 9,508 additional lives could have been saved.[1]

- In response to allegations that motorcycle helmets pose safety problems by interfering with the cyclists' hearing and peripheral vision, the NHTSA sponsored a study to determine if this is the case. The study concluded that "any negative interference of helmets on rider vision appears to be minor, especially in comparison to the protection offered by helmets should a crash occur" and that "there were no significant differences in the riders' ability to hear the auditory signals regardless of whether they were wearing a helmet or not."[2]

- Another NHTSA-sponsored study examined in detail the impact on mortality and injury rates owing to diminished use of helmets in Arkansas and Texas after those two states modified their mandatory helmet laws in 1997. The authors of the study determined that fatalities in Arkansas increased 21 percent in the first full year after the law was amended to exempt most riders, while in Texas, operator fatalities increased by 31 percent during the same period. The report further notes, "There is also good evidence that serious head injuries increased."[3]

- Helmet use saves money by reducing the incidence of serious injury. The NHTSA estimates that the use of motorcycle helmets saved $19.5 billion in health care and other costs from 1984 to 2002 and that an additional $14.8 billion would have been saved had all motorcyclists worn helmets.[4]

Before 1966, there were not any motorcycle helmet laws in any states. But then the Highway Safety Act of 1966 (PL 89-5564) significantly redefined the legal landscape. In this act, the U.S. Congress required the secretary of transportation to set uniform standards for state highway safety programs. The following year, Alan S. Boyd, the nation's first secretary of transportation, issued a directive requesting that all states enact universal helmet laws requiring that all motorcycle riders wear protective helmets. States failing to comply risked losing a portion of the federal funding allocated for highway construction. By the end of 1967, twenty-two states had enacted universal helmet laws, with fourteen more adopting similar laws the following years. By 1975, forty-seven states and the District of Columbia had enacted universal helmet laws.[5]

In 1975, the Department of Transportation made plans to withhold a portion of the federal highway funds allocated for construction in California, Illinois, and Utah, the three states that did not have universal helmet laws. (Illinois had enacted a helmet law in 1967 but repealed it in 1969 after the Illinois Supreme Court ruled that it was unconstitutional.) As word got out about the Department of Transportation's plans, Congress amended the Highway Safety Act to eliminate the secretary of transportation's authority to impose penalties on states without universal helmet laws. Within five years, more than half of the states that had enacted universal helmet laws repealed them or amended them to exempt riders over a specified age.[6]

After a period of relative stability throughout most of the 1980s, Oregon and Texas reenacted universal helmet laws in 1989, followed by Nebraska and Washington in 1990 and Maryland in 1992. Then the tide once again shifted, with Arkansas and Texas amending their universal helmet laws in 1997 to exempt many riders, followed by Kentucky in 1998.[7] The controversy continues, with helmet laws being a topic of heated debate in many state capitols.

IN LOCO PARENTIS?

Motorcycle helmets clearly save lives and reduce serious injury. Prudence and common sense suggest that wisdom is on the side of using them. But should they be required? Should the state function *in loco parentis*—as a parentlike figure mandating what is judged to be in the best interests of its citizens?

In the introduction to this volume, a distinction was made between *soft paternalism* (intervening to secure an outcome consistent with the values held by those who are being coerced) and *hard paternalism* (intervening because those doing the intervening believe they know what is best for others). The case for hard paternalism is a hard sell in a society committed to individual liberties. The claim "I know what is best for you" or "Government knows best" is a very strong one indeed—one that flies in the face of the most basic notions of liberty.

The case for soft paternalism is stronger. As also noted in the introduction, because of deficiencies in our decision-making processes or because of our failures of will, we sometimes act in ways at odds with our own deeply held values and desires, and we fail to do what these values mandate. In such cases, coercive intervention, distasteful though it might be, can have the salutary effect of forcing us to do what we in fact really want to do.

Is there a case to be made for saying that requiring people to wear helmets is consistent with their deeply held preferences? Such an argument might go roughly as follows: no one wants to be killed or seriously injured in a motorcycle accident; accordingly, requiring motorcycle riders to take measures to reduce their risk of being killed or injured is in keeping with their deeply held preferences.

This argument has a greater degree of plausibility than do arguments based on hard paternalism. However, it is by no means a foregone conclusion that the desire to reduce the risk of death or injury is in all cases greater than the desire to experience the exhilaration of riding a motorcycle without a helmet with the wind blowing in one's face. (The same is probably also true with respect to skydiving, whitewater rafting, bungee jumping, rappelling down steep mountainsides, and many other high-risk sports.)

An example from an entirely different context serves to illustrate this point. Many of us have had to deal with the agonizing decision of whether we should be supportive of aged parents who wish to continue living at home. For elderly parents who are frail, it is often the case that moving them to a well-run, adequately staffed extended-care facility could reduce risks to their health resulting from falling or failing to eat properly. In many cases, however, that's not where elderly parents want to be, even when apprised of the risks of remaining at home and the advantages of moving to an extended care facility.

I firmly believe that the wishes and preferences of elderly parents ought to be respected, as long as they stay off the highways and refrain from driving when their diminished physical capabilities pose a threat to other motorists. To force people to do things they do not want to do, even if these things would be beneficial to them, does violence to them just as surely as would physically assaulting them. To ride roughshod over deeply held personal preferences is one of the most demeaning things that can be done to anyone. It is for this reason that paternalism has little to recommend it.

COSTS IMPOSED ON OTHERS

Does an appeal to individual liberty, then, resolve the matter? Should we all jump on the repeal bandwagon, joining the effort to get rid of laws requiring motorcyclists to wear helmets?

Simple answers are often incomplete answers—and sometimes they are mistaken answers. Traumatic head injury, the incidence of which increases when motorcyclists fail to wear helmets, can be very expensive to treat, often far exceeding the financial resources of the injured individual. A study conducted by the University of Arkansas for Medical Sciences discovered that after Arkansas revised its helmet law in 1997 to exempt riders aged twenty-one years and older, unreimbursed costs related to treating those injured in motorcycle accidents increased substantially at the state's leading trauma center.[8]

It is one matter to say that engaging in risky activities is a matter for individual choice as long as the consequences are borne primarily by the perpetrator of the act. But what if significant costs are imposed on others? What if taxpayers are left with the bill? To what extent, if at all, do any of us have the right to stick others with costs that are consequences of what we freely choose to do? These are not easy questions.

To prohibit anything that inconveniences or imposes a cost on other people would result in draconian curtailments of liberty. At the same time, to ignore costs imposed on others would be exceedingly insensitive to the rights and well-being of those stuck with the bill.

Where does this leave us? When people do things that are imprudent, it is reasonable to expect them to bear the costs of their actions rather than leave these costs for others to cover. Such being the case, there is much to be said for helmet laws that exempt adult riders who have adequate health insurance to cover the cost of injury. Florida, Louisiana, and Texas have moved in this direction, though there is room for debate about what constitutes adequate coverage.[9] But regardless of how this matter is resolved, such helmet laws have much to recommend them.[10] They recognize both the importance of individual choice and limits as to the extent that we can expect others to pick up the tab for our choices. Perhaps as the debate about helmet laws continues, a balanced approach of this sort can bring constructive resolution to a divisive issue.

SOME CONCLUDING CONSIDERATIONS

As noted in the introduction, just war theorists insist that all relevant criteria be satisfied before intervention is justifiable—namely, just cause, right intent, last resort, lawful authority, reasonable hope of success, and due proportionality. In the introduction and in this chapter, I have argued that paternalism is not a sufficient reason for intervention.

The case for intervention is stronger when the well-being of others is at risk. Since the expenses related to treating head injuries suffered by unhelmeted riders can place the well-being of others at risk by eroding their financial resources, a modest case can be made for requiring that riders who choose not to wear helmets carry sufficient insurance to cover the cost of treating their injuries—provided, of course, that the criteria of right intent, last resort, lawful authority, reasonable hope of success, and due proportionality are met. Insofar as I can determine, mandatory insurance laws satisfy all of these criteria.

NOTES

1. U.S. National Highway Traffic Safety Administration (NHTSA), *Traffic Safety Facts: Motorcycle Helmet Use Laws* (April 2004), 1, at www.nhtsa.dot .gov/people/injury/New-fact-sheet03/MotorcycleHelmet.pdf.

2. NHTSA, *Traffic Tech: Technology Transfer Series*, no. 127, June 1996.

3. D. F. Preusser, J. H. Hedlund, and R. G. Ulmer, *Evaluation of Motorcycle Helmet Law Repeal in Arkansas and Texas* (NHTSA, 2000), vi–x.

4. NHTSA, *Motorcycle Helmet Use Laws*, 3.

5. Preusser, Hedlund, and Ulmer, *Motorcycle Helmet Law Repeal*, 2.

6. Preusser, Hedlund, and Ulmer, *Motorcycle Helmet Law Repeal*, 3.

7. Preusser, Hedlund, and Ulmer, *Motorcycle Helmet Law Repeal*, 4–5.

8. Rodney Bowers, *Arkansas Democrat-Gazette*, February 25, 2002, B1.

9. Florida's helmet law exempts riders twenty-one years of age and older who have health insurance with at least $10,000 in medical benefits for injuries resulting from a motorcycle crash, while Texas's law makes similar provisions but adds the requirement that a rider-training course be completed. In Louisiana, the exemption is for riders eighteen years of age and older with proof of health insurance with medical benefits of at least $10,000. Kentucky had an insurance requirement, but this provision was repealed effective July 15, 2000 (NHTSA, *Motorcycle Helmet Use Laws*, 8–9).

10. I am indebted to my daughter, Elizabeth J. Lee, for bringing to my attention an argument that cuts the other direction. She notes that if a motorcycle rider who was not wearing a helmet were struck by another vehicle and died as a result of injuries sustained, the driver of that vehicle could be charged with homicide rather than the lesser charges that would result if the motorcycle rider were wearing a helmet and survived the accident. She is, of course, right about that. However, is protecting intoxicated and other irresponsible drivers from more serious charges a sufficient reason for curtailing the liberty of motorcycle riders? I am not convinced that it is.

Ten Questions for Reflection and Discussion

1   What are reasons that some motorcycle riders might choose not to wear helmets? Are these plausible reasons?

2   What are reasons for wearing a helmet when riding a motorcycle? Which are more persuasive— the reasons for wearing a helmet or the reasons for not wearing a helmet?

3   Do people have a right to act imprudently, provided that they are the ones who suffer the consequences of their action? Is riding a motorcycle without wearing a helmet such a right?

4   To what extent, if at all, is paternalism a sufficient reason for intervening in the lives of other people if they are inclined to act imprudently?

5   Is requiring motorcycle riders to wear helmets justifiable?

6   To what extent, if at all, is the case stronger for requiring motorcycle riders under of the age of eighteen to wear helmets than it is for requiring adult riders to wear helmets?

7   What might be done to persuade motorcycle riders to voluntarily wear helmets?

8   If adult riders who choose not to wear helmets were to be required to have sufficient medical insurance to cover the cost of treating possible injury, how much insurance is enough?

9   When viewed from an ethical perspective, what is the difference, if any, between mandatory helmet laws and mandatory seat belt laws?

10   Given that individuals who die from traumatic head injuries are prime candidates for organ donation, should motorcycle riders with signed organ donor cards be exempt from mandatory helmet laws?

2

PHYSICIAN-ASSISTED SUICIDE

—

In the course of the years, my views with respect to the morality of physician-assisted suicide have not wavered one bit. I'm opposed to it. Strongly opposed to it. I agree with Karl Barth that "it is for God and God alone to make an end of human life" and that God gives life to us "as an inalienable loan."[1] I believe that meaning and hope are possible in all of life's situations, even in the midst of suffering.[2] I am very uncomfortable with the idea of physicians, who are trained to preserve life, dispensing lethal drugs to be used to end life. Insofar as the morality of physician-assisted suicide is concerned, I find myself solidly in the conservative camp.

In recent years, however, as Oregon has legalized physician-assisted suicide[3] and as other states have considered doing so,[4] I have found myself wrestling with a very difficult question. Do those of us with deep moral reservations about the morality of physician-assisted suicide have any business using the coercive power of government to prevent those who disagree from doing what they believe is right? Are there any compelling arguments to justify placing legal roadblocks in the way of terminally ill individuals who wish to end their suffering by ending their lives, provided such decisions are made only after thoughtful, careful deliberation in an environment devoid of social pressure?

As noted in the introduction, when what some might do poses a significant risk to the health and well-being of others, a strong case can be made for intervention to protect those who are threatened. But does that rationale work in the case of physician-assisted suicide? Protecting vulnerable individuals from threats posed by others is one matter. But what if the consequences of the act are borne primarily by the perpetrator of the act, as is the case with physician-assisted suicide?

Does some form of paternalism provide adequate grounds for intervention—intervention rationalized as being in the best interest of the person being restrained? Does the "slippery slope" argument provide an adequate rationale for intervention by suggesting that physician-assisted suicide will lead to other sorts of abuses? These are neither easy nor insignificant questions.

WHEN ARE WE JUSTIFIED IN INTERVENING TO PREVENT OTHERS FROM HARMING THEMSELVES?

As noted in the introduction, social philosopher Joel Feinberg, commenting on John Stuart Mill's strong defense of individual liberty, observes, "Nevertheless, there are some actions that create a powerful presumption that an actor in his right mind would not choose them." The stronger the presumption, "the more elaborate and fastidious should be the legal paraphernalia required, and the stricter the standards of evidence" if that presumption is to be overridden. He concludes, "The point of the procedure would not be to evaluate the wisdom or worthiness of a person's choice, but rather to determine whether the choice really is his." And what of suicide? Feinberg comments, "The desire to commit suicide must always be presumed to be both nonvoluntary and harmful to others until shown otherwise. (Of course, in some cases it can be shown otherwise.)"[5]

There is a good deal of wisdom in Feinberg's approach. Suicide and attempted suicide often are acts of desperation by individuals who, as a result of mental illness or other distorting factors, are not in full command of their senses. In such cases, an ethic dedicated to the preservation of human life and affirming the dignity of each person mandates intervention to prevent self-destruction.

But, as Feinberg allows, it is also possible that in some cases suicide really is a freely chosen course of action by those in full command of their senses. In advocating "elaborate and fastidious" legal procedures to assess situations such as these, he emphasizes that "the point of the procedure would not be to evaluate the wisdom or worthiness of a person's choice, but rather to determine whether the choice really is his."

The Oregon Death with Dignity Act specifies an elaborate procedure that must be followed before anyone can be given lethal drugs to be self-administered. The procedural safeguards include the following:

- To request a prescription for lethal medications, the requesting individual must be a resident of Oregon, eighteen years of age or older, and capable of making health care decisions, defined as being present when "in the opinion of a court or in the opinion of the patient's attending physician or consulting physician, psychiatrist or psychologist, a patient has the ability to make and communicate health care decisions to providers."

- The requesting individual must be diagnosed as having a terminal illness that will lead to death within six months.

- To receive medication, the terminally ill individual must make two oral requests to his or her physician, separated by at least fifteen days, and provide a written request to the physician, witnessed by two witnesses; at least one witness must be someone who is not a relative of the person initiating the request, who is

13

not entitled to any portion of the person's estate upon death, and who is not the owner, operator, or an employee of a health care facility where the person is a patient or a resident.

- Before issuing a prescription for lethal medication, both the prescribing physician and a consulting physician must determine whether the patient is capable of making health care decisions and must confirm both the diagnosis and the prognosis; if either physician believes that the patient's decision-making capability is impaired by a psychiatric or psychological disorder, he or she must refer the patient for a psychological examination.

- Before prescribing lethal medications, the prescribing physician must inform the terminally ill individual of alternatives to suicide, "including, but not limited to, comfort care, hospice care and pain control."

- The prescribing physician must inform the patient that he or she will have the opportunity to rescind the request at any time and in any manner; the law further provides that when the patient makes his or her second oral request, the physician shall offer the patient the opportunity to rescind the request.

- In addition to the fifteen-day waiting period between a patient's two oral requests for lethal medication, there must be a waiting period of forty-eight hours between a patient's written request and the writing of a prescription.

With procedural safeguards such as these in place, it is difficult, if not impossible, to envision any situation in which physician-assisted suicide in Oregon, if done consistently within the standards stated in the Death with Dignity Act, would not satisfy the most rigorous standards of voluntariness. In *On Liberty*, John Stuart Mills cautions, "A person should be free to do as he likes in his own concerns, but he ought not be free to do as he likes in acting for another, under the pre-text that the affairs of the other are his own affairs."[6] In short, whether we like what others might be inclined to do is one matter. Quite an-other is whether we have any business intervening in their affairs as long as the costs of what they are doing are borne primarily by the per-petrator of the act.

IS PHYSICIAN-ASSISTED SUICIDE A SLIPPERY SLOPE?

What about the slippery-slope argument? Might legalizing physician-assisted suicide lead to all sorts of abuses? To assess the validity of the slippery-slope argument, we need to inquire what undesirable state of affairs awaits those who "slide down."

In the heated debate about the legalization of physician-assisted sui-cide, there are actually two variations of the slippery-slope argument. One variation warns that allowing physician-assisted suicide could re-sult in social pressures on the aged and the infirm, compelling them to exercise this option. Several years ago, then governor Richard Lamm of Colorado stirred up a storm of controversy when he was quoted as say-ing that there is "a duty to die and get out of the way."[7] Those were shocking words then, and they continue to be shocking words today. In an article that appeared in *Christianity Today* shortly after Oregon le-galized physician-assisted suicide, Peter J. Bernardi, assistant professor of religious studies at Loyola University in New Orleans, warned that "the right to die may become the duty to die." He argued, "Radical au-tonomy is a deadly deception. Proponents of mercy killing argue for the right of mentally competent, terminally ill adults to receive a physi-cian's assistance to commit suicide. The reality is that such autonomous requests will be subtly or not so subtly influenced by others."[8]

Social pressure pushing suffering individuals in the direction of physician-assisted suicide would be highly objectionable. But is such pressure unavoidable, as the critics of physician-assisted suicide seem to believe? Along with ensuring the highest level of rationality possible in the decision-making process, the provisions of the Oregon law are intended make it very clear to those contemplating suicide that they are under no pressure to do so. For example, the requirement that physicians, before prescribing lethal medications, must inform terminally ill individuals requesting such medications about hospice care and other alternatives is a way of saying, "Look, you don't have to do this. There are other options." And the requirement that there be multiple opportunities to rescind the request, including an explicitly stated opportunity at the end of the fifteen-day waiting period, is a way of saying, "Are you sure you really want to do this?" In short, legalizing physician-assisted suicide need not translate into a suggestion that there is a duty to die. If physician-assisted suicide is presented as an option that no one need exercise, it then remains a matter of individual choice rather than a decision forced or encouraged by social pressure.

A second variation of the slippery-slope argument warns that voluntary physician-assisted suicide invites abuses such as physicians taking it upon themselves to end the lives of terminally ill patients. Daniel Callahan has reported that in the Netherlands (where physician-assisted suicide has been practiced for a number of years) "there are a substantial number of cases of nonvoluntary euthanasia, that is, euthanasia undertaken without the explicit permission of the person being killed."[9]

Like many others, I find nonvoluntary euthanasia morally reprehensible. But does physician-assisted suicide inevitably lead in this direction? Supporters of legalizing physician-assisted suicide frequently contend that rigorous safeguards, such as those incorporated in the Oregon law, can prevent nonvoluntary euthanasia by ensuring that euthanasia occurs only at the request of the suffering individual. Their arguments are persuasive.

There is, it might be added, another firewall—one built into the Oregon law—that might be even more significant: requiring that lethal drugs be self-administered rather than administered by the prescribing physician or anyone else. If physicians, family members, and others are prohibited from administering lethal drugs to terminally ill patients and if that restriction is rigorously enforced, nonvoluntary euthanasia is precluded.

Those who make the slippery-slope argument often cite the Dutch experience as a warning of what might happen if physician-assisted suicide is allowed. But how relevant is the Dutch experience? It should be noted that until the Dutch Parliament legalized physician-assisted suicide in April 2001,[10] all forms of active euthanasia were technically illegal in the Netherlands, even though legal authorities often looked the other way when physicians prescribed lethal medications for terminally ill patients.[11] A widespread practice that functions outside of the law is by its very nature difficult to regulate, and it inevitably invites abuse. In short, legalizing physician-assisted suicide and carefully regulating its practice might be a more effective way of preventing a slide down a slippery slope leading to nonvoluntary active euthanasia than would continuing the legal prohibition on physician-assisted suicide.

Finally, it is of significance that to date the Oregon experience in no way suggests that a slide down a slippery slope is imminent. Oregon's Death with Dignity Act has been used sparingly. The number of Oregonians opting for physician-assisted suicide has ranged from sixteen in 1998, the first year the law was in effect, to forty-two in 2003. While this might appear to be a sizable increase, the cases of physician-assisted suicide represent a very small fraction of the total number of deaths in Oregon. As noted in the most recent report of the Oregon Department of Human Services, the 171 deaths from physician-assisted suicide since the inception of the act are only a minuscule portion of the total number of deaths (53,544) in Oregon from the same diseases during the same period. Put in percentage terms, the deaths from physician-assisted suicide account for 0.3 percent of the Oregon deaths from the diseases experienced by those who opted for physician-assisted suicide. Clearly, there is no landslide in the making. Moreover, there is little data, if any, to substantiate the allegation that the Oregon law fosters "a duty to die." The Oregon Department of Human Resources reports that the reasons most frequently given by patients for requesting lethal medication are loss of autonomy (87 percent), diminished ability to do things that make life enjoyable (83 percent), and loss of dignity (82 percent). Only 36 percent gave as a reason burden on family, friends, and caregivers. (Since many patients gave multiple reasons for requesting lethal medication, the percentages add up to more than 100 percent.)[12]

SOME CONCLUDING CONSIDERATIONS

In the introduction, I note six criteria drawn from just war theory, all of which must be satisfied to make a case for coercive intervention: just cause, right intent, last resort, lawful authority, reasonable hope of success, and due proportionality. If paternalism does not constitute a just cause for intervention, then no case can be made for coercive intervention in situations in which terminally ill patients in full command of their senses wish to end their suffering by ending their lives. Though some of us might firmly believe that physicians ought to preserve life rather than assist in ending life, there is likewise no compelling case for "throwing the law" at physicians willing to prescribe lethal medications for patients wishing to end their suffering by ending their lives.

Thus when all things are considered, the arguments in favor of continuing to prohibit physician-assisted suicide are not particularly compelling. This is not to suggest that those of us who are of a more conservative persuasion should spearhead legalization campaigns. But it does suggest that we should not stand in the way of thoughtful individuals such as prominent physician Timothy Quill[13] and former *New England Journal of Medicine* editor Marcia Angell,[14] both of whom favor legalization.[15]

Those of us opposed to physician-assisted suicide would do well to focus our efforts on helping others discover the meaning and hope that are possible in life, even in the midst of suffering. We can accomplish far more by reaching out in a loving, caring manner to those experiencing great suffering, instead of sitting around moralizing about what they should or should not do and threatening physicians with legal penalties if they act in ways at odds with values we hold dear. If we were to respond effectively with love and compassion, then physician-assisted suicide would likely be an option rarely, if ever, chosen.[16]

NOTES

1. Karl Barth, *Church Dogmatics,* vol. 3, *The Doctrine of Creation,* part 4, ed. B. W. Bromily and T. F. Torrance, tr. A. T. Mackay et al. (Edinburgh: T & T Clark, 1961), 404, 425.

2. See, for example, the Evangelical Lutheran Church in America message, *End-of-Life Decisions* (Chicago: Division for Church in Society, Evangelical Lutheran Church in America, 1992), which states that "hope and meaning in life are possible even in times of suffering and adversity" (2). The statement is a quotation from a social statement on death and dying adopted in 1982 by the Lutheran Church in America, one of the groups that merged to form the Evangelical Lutheran Church in America in 1988.

3. The Oregon Death with Dignity Act is a citizen's initiative passed by Oregon voters in 1994 and reaffirmed by Oregon voters three years later. The full text of the act is available online at www.ohd.hr.state.or.us/chs/pas/ors.htm.

4. In the November 2000 general election, voters in Maine narrowly rejected a measure similar to that approved by Oregon voters (Carey Goldberg, "Campaign Briefing: Assisted Suicide Vote," *New York Times,* October 28, 2000, A13, and "The 2000 Election: Maine," *New York Times,* November 9, 2000, B14). In Hawaii, two bills that would legalize physician-assisted suicide were approved by the state's House of Representatives. The bills, however, have encountered opposition in the state senate (Bruce Dunford, "Matsuura Bottles Up Death with Dignity Bill," Associated Press, March 23, 2002, and B. J. Reyes, "Assisted Suicide Measure Advances in State House," Associated Press, March 5, 2004). In Vermont, a bill legalizing physician-assisted suicide has

been bottled up in committee (Anne Wallace Allen, "Assisted Suicide Advocates Looking to Next Year," Associated Press, May 18, 2004).

5. Joel Feinberg, *Social Philosophy* (Englewood Cliffs, N.J.: Prentice-Hall, 1973), 49–51.

6. John Stuart Mill, *On Liberty*, ed. Currin V. Shields (Indianapolis, Ind.: Bobbs-Merrill, 1956), 127.

7. Quoted in "Gov. Lamm Asserts Elderly, If Very Ill, Have 'Duty to Die,'" *New York Times*, March 29, 1984, sec. I, 16. The quotation reportedly came from a speech Governor Lamm gave at a meeting of the Colorado Health Lawyers Association at St. Joseph's Hospital in Denver. He may have been quoted out of context. In an editorial that ran two days later, the *New York Times* suggested that "Governor Lamm's fast-moving tongue was off, but his mind was in the right place." The editorial theorized that the point that Governor Lamm was attempting to make is that there is a limit to how much high-cost, high-tech medical treatment any of us can expect others to provide for us. The editorial stated, "He was speaking of the terminally ill of any age, of an extraordinarily expensive medical technology that has developed faster than a corresponding ethic and of the financial implications for a nation that picks up much of the bill" ("Life, Death, and Governor Lamm," *New York Times*, March 31, 1984, sec. I, 22).

8. Peter J. Bernardi, "Is Death a Right?" *Christianity Today* 40 (May 20, 1996): 29–30.

9. Daniel Callahan, "When Self-Determination Runs Amok," *Hastings Center Report* (March–April 1992): 52–55. There is some data to back up Callahan's claim. The Remmelink report, an official Dutch government study of the practice of euthanasia in the Netherlands, indicates that in 1990, doctors actively killed 1,040 patients without their knowledge or consent, at www.euthanasia.com/hollchart.html (accessed March 25, 2002).

10. "Legalized Euthanasia, Assisted Suicide Get Parliament's OK in the Netherlands; Law Makes Nation First to Take Such Action," *St. Louis Post-Dispatch*, April 11, 2001, A2.

11. In an article entitled "After the Slippery Slope: Dutch Experiences on Regulating Active Euthanasia," Theo A. Boer, who teaches at Utrecht University, comments, "Perhaps Dutch experiences in the euthanasia debate indicate that in an open and democratic society, self-corrective mechanisms may prevent many slippery slope nightmares from becoming true. Perhaps they prove that when euthanasia becomes legal, some unwanted or unexpected side-effects cannot be excluded. Perhaps they give reasons for caution in following the Dutch example"

("After the Slippery Slope: Dutch Experiences on Regulating Active Euthanasia," *Journal of the Society of Christian Ethics* 23, no. 2 [Fall/Winter 2003]: 239). As Boer notes, the Dutch law enacted in April 2001 allows not only assisted suicide but also termination of life at the request of the patient. Thus, the Dutch law does not have the firewall like the one built into the Oregon law—that of requiring that the lethal drugs be self-administered rather than administered by the prescribing physician or someone else. The Dutch law continues to be the center of considerable controversy. See, for example, Keith B. Richburg, "Death with Dignity, or Door to Abuse? Popular Dutch Euthanasia Law Continues to Draw Condemnation," *Washington Post*, January 4, 2004, A1.

12. Detailed statistics on the Oregon experience are included in *Oregon's Death with Dignity Act Annual Report 2003* issued by the Oregon Department of Human Resources, at www.dhs.state.or.us/publichealth/chs/pas/ar-index.cfm (accessed August 23, 2004).

13. One of the most poignant presentations of the case for physician-assisted suicide is found in a widely read and frequently reprinted article by Timothy E. Quill entitled "Death and Dignity: A Case of Individualized Decision Making," which first appeared in the *New England Journal of Medicine* 324 (March 7, 1991): 691–94 (included in *Bioethics,* 4th edition, ed. Thomas A. Shannon [Mahwah, N.J.: Paulist Press, 1992], 167–72). See also Timothy E. Quill, Christine K. Cassel, and Diane E. Meier, "Care of the Hopelessly Ill: Proposed Criteria for Physician-Assisted Suicide," *New England Journal of Medicine* 327 (November 5, 1992): 1381–83, and Franklin G. Miller, Timothy E. Quill, Howard Brody, John C. Fletcher, Lawrence O. Gostin, and Diane E. Meier, "Regulating Physician-Assisted Suicide," *New England Journal of Medicine* 331 (July 14, 1994): 119–23.

14. See, for example, Marcia Angell, "No Choice but to Die Alone," *Washington Post*, February 24, 2002, B7. She observes, "It seems to me that Oregon has chosen a path that gives dying patients the opportunity to exercise the greatest possible self-determination with the full support of their families and communities."

15. It might be added that no one really knows what end-of-life situations involving immense suffering are like until he or she experiences them firsthand.

16. This chapter is a substantially expanded version of an article that first appeared in the *Hastings Center Report* (Daniel E. Lee, "Physician-Assisted Suicide: A Conservative Critique," *Hastings Center Report* 33, no. 1 [January–February 2003]: 17–19).

Ten Questions for Reflection and Discussion

1. Is suicide ever a rational decision?

2. In what situations, if any, is suicide a morally acceptable option?

3. If suicide is sometimes morally acceptable, why is it morally acceptable? If it is never morally acceptable, why is it not morally acceptable?

4. Should terminally ill patients experiencing immense suffering be allowed to end their suffering by ending their lives?

5. Should physicians be allowed to prescribe lethal medications for patients requesting such medications?

6   Should physicians be allowed to administer lethal medications to patients requesting such medications?

7   Should other states enact laws similar to the Oregon Death with Dignity Act?

8   Does physician-assisted suicide place one on a slippery slope that undermines respect for human life in other situations?

9   Does the Oregon Death with Dignity Act include adequate safeguards to prevent abuse?

10 What are some alternatives to physician-assisted suicide? How might utilization of these alternatives be encouraged?

3

RECREATIONAL USE OF MARIJUANA

—

I find the question of whether recreational use of marijuana should be legalized a very difficult matter. I agree with the apostle Paul that our bodies are temples of the Holy Spirit (*I Corinthians* 6.19–20) and believe that to use mind-altering drugs simply for whatever thrill they might impart is to be disrespectful of this temple.[1] I further believe that the richness and goodness of life are so immense that there is no need for mind-altering drugs to experience exhilaration or an emotional high. But do I or anyone else have any business trying to prevent others from using marijuana if they so desire?[2]

There are, to be sure, some situations in which we would all agree that the use of mind-altering drugs ought to be prohibited. While flying, we do not want airline pilots to be high (in more ways than one), and during surgery, we would vastly prefer that surgeons be in full command of their senses. But what about the recreational use of marijuana in the privacy of one's home in situations that do not pose any threats to anyone else's health or safety?[3] That's a far more difficult matter.

There is a libertarian argument that suggests that if those who have attained the age of majority wish to smoke marijuana in the privacy of their own homes, that is their business, not ours. In testimony presented to a congressional subcommittee, R. Keith Stroup, executive director of the National Organization for the Reform of Marijuana Laws (NORML)—one of the leading advocacy groups favoring legalization—stated, "Most would agree that the government has no business knowing what books we read, the subject of our telephone conversations, or how we conduct ourselves in the bedroom. Similarly, whether one smokes marijuana or drinks alcohol to relax is simply not an appropriate area of concern for the government."[4]

The libertarian argument is, at least at first glance, plausible. And it is consistent with arguments that have been made in previous chapters with respect to physician-assisted suicide and motorcycle helmets. There is, however, more to the matter. In commenting on physician-assisted suicide, I expressed concern that social pressure might cause some to act injudiciously and that safeguards, such as those specified by the Oregon law, need to be in place to keep this from happening. There is even greater cause for concern with respect to the recreational use of marijuana. Almost all of those who might be inclined to consider physician-assisted suicide attained the age of majority years ago. The same is not true of those who might be attracted to the recreational use of marijuana. As in the case of underage drinking, considerable peer pressure can and often does push teenagers and others in the direction of using drugs. Legalizing marijuana for adults, and thereby making it more readily available in general, risks increasing this peer pressure.[5]

UTILITARIAN ARGUMENTS

Some argue the case for legalization on utilitarian grounds. Among those approaching the issue in this way is that well-known icon of conservatism, William F. Buckley Jr. In an issue of *National Review* devoted to the question of whether drug use should be decriminalized, he recalls his intellectual odyssey with respect to this particular issue:

I came to the conclusion that the so-called war against drugs was not working, that it would not work absent a change in the structure of the civil rights to which we are accustomed and to which we cling as a valuable part of our patrimony. And that therefore if that war against drugs is not working we should look into what effects the war has, a canvass of the casualties consequent on its failure to work. That consideration encouraged me to weigh utilitarian principles: the Benthamite calculus of pain and pleasure introduced by the illegalization of drugs. . . . More people die every year as a result of the war against drugs than die from what we call, generically, overdosing. These fatalities include, most prominently, drug merchants who compete for commercial territory, but also people who are robbed and killed by those desperate for money to buy the drug to which they have become addicted.[6]

Buckley further suggests that the economic costs, direct and indirect, of the war on drugs are also considerable and outweigh any benefits that might be derived from efforts to curtail the use of drugs.[7] In the introduction to this volume, I note that reasonable hope of success and due proportionality (the good that results must outweigh the costs) have played a significant role in traditional just war theory. In effect, Buckley has concluded that efforts to suppress drug use fail to satisfy these two criteria.

It bears noting that Buckley advocates legalization of all illicit drugs, presumably including heroin and cocaine, not just marijuana. This raises a rather sticky question for those favoring legalization of marijuana. In practice, would legalization of marijuana prove to be the first step toward legalization of cocaine and heroin? And if so, is this really the direction we want to head?

In making economic arguments in favor of legalization, Buckley gives scant attention to the economic costs that might accompany the legalization of powerfully addictive drugs such as cocaine and heroin, costs that include loss of productivity and increased dependence on public aid resulting from inability to hold a job. The carrying costs resulting from addiction to cocaine and heroin are already considerable.

Would not legalization of such drugs increase these social costs? The social costs of addiction to alcohol, which is legal, are substantial, even with a plethora of programs intended to reduce the incidence of alcohol abuse. Is there any reason to believe that legalization of cocaine and heroin would reduce the social costs associated with the use of these drugs? When one takes into account the carrying costs of noncontributing members of society resulting from drug addiction, might not these costs actually increase?

A GATEWAY DRUG?

The arguments in favor of continuing the prohibition of the recreational use of marijuana are no more compelling. One of the most common arguments—one that is made sooner or later by just about everyone who favors continued prohibition—holds that marijuana use is the first step down a deadly road of addiction leading to the use of cocaine, heroin, and other powerfully addictive drugs. A newspaper article that appeared in the *San Jose Mercury News* paints the following picture: "Madeleine started with marijuana . . . then moved on to alcohol and cocaine. For 28 years she used and abused drugs, losing her marriage, children, and nearly half her life in the process."[8] A widely used reference book on drugs and addictive behavior states,

> Since about 1950 . . . smoking of marijuana has been linked statistically to the use of other illegal drugs, such as heroin and cocaine. Most observers have concluded that the link is sociological rather than biological, and that the use of marijuana is a marker for individuals who are more prone to seek new experiences even when these violate social norms and local laws. Further, the process of obtaining illegal marijuana increases the likelihood of contact with dealers and other individuals who have access to drugs such as heroin. Consequently, marijuana has been referred to as a "gateway" drug, one whose use often leads to the use of other illegal drugs.[9]

A report issued in 1994 by Columbia University's Center on Addiction and Substance Abuse asserts that "children 12–17 years old who use marijuana are 85 times more likely . . . to use cocaine than children who never used a gateway drug."[10]

Whether marijuana actually functions as a "gateway" drug is open to question, though. In *Marihuana: A Signal of Misunderstanding*, a report issued by the federal government over three decades ago, the National Commission on Marihuana and Drug Abuse (the commission used the alternate spelling of *marijuana*) stated:

> Citizens concerned with health issues must consider the possibility of marihuana use leading to use of heroin, other opiates, cocaine or hallucinogens. This so-called stepping-stone theory first received widespread acceptance in 1951 as a result of testimony at Congressional hearings. At that time, studies of various addict populations repeatedly described most heroin users as marihuana users also. The implication of these descriptions was that a causal relationship existed between marihuana and subsequent heroin use. When the voluminous testimony given at these hearings is seriously examined, no verification is found of a causal relationship between marihuana use and subsequent heroin use.[11]

The commission further stated that "marihuana use per se does not dictate whether other drugs will be used; nor does it determine the rate of progression, if and when it occurs, or which drugs might be used."[12]

A causal link, if such exists, between marijuana use and addiction to drugs such as heroin and cocaine is difficult to document. Granted, as is often noted, many of those who use cocaine and heroin used marijuana before moving on to cocaine and heroin. However, as statisticians correctly remind us, correlation does not establish causality. In a book published in 1996, Harvard geologist and zoologist Stephen Jay Gould observes that in the preceding ten years, both the price of gasoline and his age increased. However, that does not in any way suggest that one had anything to do with the other. He concludes, "The invalid assumption that correlation implies cause is probably among the two or three most serious and common errors of human reasoning."[13] John P. Morgan, a professor of pharmacology at City University of New York Medical School who rejects the "gateway" theory, observes, "Most people who ride a motorcycle have ridden a bicycle. However, bicycle riding does not cause motorcycle riding."[14]

In short, the fact that many who are addicted to heroin and crack cocaine have used marijuana does not substantiate the claim that use of marijuana leads to the use of heroin or other powerful addictive drugs. Even if marijuana users are more likely to use heroin and cocaine than nonusers are, that does not prove causation. Rather, what it might signify is that those who habitually break the law in some areas are likely to do so in other areas, in which case legalizing marijuana might have the salutary effect of reducing use of heroin and cocaine.

At the same time, while the evidence is far from compelling, it is possible that there is a link—psychological, sociological, or otherwise—between the use of marijuana and the use of heroin and cocaine. That is why wisdom favors further study before we rush headlong in the direction of legalization. There is tremendous need for unbiased research in this area.

A link, if such exists, between marijuana and other drugs might be indirect rather than direct. Troubled adolescents with antisocial tendencies are more likely to become dependent on marijuana than are adolescents without these tendencies.[15] Personal problems and difficulties in relating to others are widely believed to be contributing factors to cocaine and heroin use. If personal problems lead troubled adolescents and others to seek the escapism of mind-altering drugs, it should surprise no one to discover that a far higher percentage of marijuana users use cocaine or heroin than do those who have never used marijuana. However, this in no way would substantiate the claim that using marijuana leads to use of cocaine or heroin. Nor does it necessarily suggest that curtailing marijuana use would result in lower usage rates for cocaine and heroin. Rather, it suggests that a key to reducing the use of cocaine and heroin is resolving the personal problems that move troubled adolescents and others to seek escape in mind-altering drugs.

AN ADDICTIVE DRUG?

But what about marijuana itself? Is it an addictive drug? Does it result in chemical dependency that deprives users of the freedom to choose not to use it? There is no consensus on this matter. In *Marihuana: A Signal of Misunderstanding*, the National Commission on Marihuana and Drug Abuse states,

> Unfortunately, fact and fancy have become irrationally mixed regarding marihuana's physiological and psychological properties. Marihuana clearly is not in the same chemical category as heroin insofar as its physiologic and psychological effects are concerned. In a word, cannabis does not lead to physical dependence. No torturous withdrawal syndrome follows the sudden cessation of chronic, heavy use of marihuana. Although evidence indicates that heavy, long-term cannabis users may develop psychological dependence, even then the level of psychological dependence is no different from the syndrome of anxiety and restlessness seen when an American stops smoking tobacco cigarettes.[16]

It might be added that in recent years, numerous studies have suggested that the nicotine in tobacco products can result in chemical dependency. Thus, the comparison to smoking tobacco cigarettes might not rule out chemical dependency. Also of possible significance is a recent federal study conducted by Steven Goldberg for the National Institute on Drug Abuse in which four squirrel monkeys repeatedly dosed themselves with THC (tetrahydrocannabinol, the active ingredient in marijuana), which led the institute to conclude that marijuana is addictive.[17] In a pamphlet entitled *Marijuana: Facts for Teens*, the institute responds emphatically to the question of whether people can become addicted to marijuana:

> Yes. While not everyone who uses marijuana becomes addicted, when a user begins to seek out and take the drug compulsively, that person is said to be dependent or addicted to the drug. In 1995, 165,000 people entering drug treatment programs reported marijuana as their primary drug of abuse.

Others, however, sharply disagree. Dr. Lester Grinspoon, a Harvard Medical School emeritus professor of psychiatry who chairs the board of the NORML foundation, says of marijuana, "This drug is not addicting. Clinical experience says that."[18]

SOME CONCLUDING CONSIDERATIONS

How does all of this sort out with respect to the criteria for intervention derived from just war theory (noted in the introduction)? Lawful authority poses no particular difficulties, but what about the other criteria?

- *Just cause:* There is just cause for intervention if marijuana is an addictive drug that leads to use of cocaine, heroin, and other drugs that impose substantial social costs. But is it?

- *Right intent:* Does the intent behind prohibition efforts reflect a concern about the well-being of those whose lives might be adversely affected by drug use? Or is it primarily because those favoring prohibition do not like drugs?

- *Last resort:* Are there effective ways of discouraging drug use short of coercive intervention?

- *Reasonable hope of success:* Does prohibition work?

- *Due proportionality:* Is whatever benefit that might be derived from prohibiting recreational use of marijuana sufficient to offset the costs of prohibition efforts?

Just war theorists have traditionally argued that if the case for military intervention is not conclusive, one ought not intervene. When applied to the recreational use of marijuana, this might be construed as suggesting that if the arguments for intervention are not compelling, laws prohibiting recreational use of marijuana ought to be repealed.

However, one can also make an argument for maintaining the status quo while seeking answers to the unanswered questions. In the current political climate, efforts to legalize the recreational use of marijuana would be met with a firestorm of controversy making that of physician-assisted suicide seem mild by comparison. If prohibition laws were repealed and if subsequent research were to later indicate compelling reasons for prohibition, it would then be necessary to go through a grueling political process to reinstate prohibition laws.

In short, it is within the range of the possible that at some point in the future, there will be persuasive arguments supporting legalization of recreational use of marijuana. That time has not yet come. It is also possible, however, that additional research will support continued prohibition. For the time being, it makes sense to maintain the status quo while seeking answers to the unanswered questions.[19]

NOTES

1. Compare John Jefferson Davis, "Biblical Authority," in *Moral Issues and Christian Response*, 6th ed., ed. Paul T. Jersild, Dale A. Johnson, Patricia Beattie Jung, and Shannon Jung (Fort Worth, Tex.: Harcourt, Brace, 1998), 29–33. Davis states, "Cocaine abuse, for example, while not explicitly addressed in the Bible, is certainly inconsistent with the teaching that the body is the temple of the Holy Spirit and is not to be abused" (31).

2. In the United States, the use of marijuana was not prohibited until 1937, at which time Congress passed legislation listing marijuana as a "narcotic drug." In the Comprehensive Drug Abuse Prevention and Control Act of 1970, Congress established a thirteen-member commission to study and make recommendations with respect to drug-related issues. In March 1972, the commission issued its report on marijuana, entitled *Marihuana: A Signal of Misunderstanding*. (The full text is available at www.druglibrary.org/schaffer/library/studies/nc/ncmenu.htm.) The commission recommended that federal law be changed to provide that "possession of marihuana for personal use would no longer be an offense, but marihuana possessed in public would remain contraband subject to summary seizure and forfeiture." The commission further recommended that "casual distribution of small amounts of marihuana for no remuneration, or insignificant remuneration not involving profit would no longer be an offense." President Richard M. Nixon, who had appointed nine of the commission members, disavowed the recommendation. In 1973, Oregon became the first state to decriminalize possession of small amounts of marijuana. In subsequent years, several other states eliminated incarceration as a penalty for simple possession, in many cases substituting a modest fine. For a concise overview of the legal history of marijuana prohibition in the United States, see Richard J. Bonnie, "Marihuana Commission: Recommendations on Decriminalization," in *Encyclopedia of Drugs, Alcohol and Addictive Behavior*, 2nd ed., vol. 2 (New York: Macmillan Reference, 2001), 700–702.

3. There is some data suggesting that marijuana poses health risks for those who use it. In a pamphlet entitled *Marijuana: Facts for Teens,* www.nida.nih.gov/MarijBroch/Marijteenstxt.html, the National Institute on Drug Abuse lists problems with the respiratory and immune systems as possible consequences of smoking marijuana. That, however, is not the issue at stake here. Rather, it is whether those who are willing to assume those risks should be allowed to use marijuana in the privacy of their homes or in other situations that do not pose risks to others.

4. Testimony of R. Keith Stroup, Esq., executive director, NORML, before the Subcommittee on Criminal Justice, Drug Policy, and Human Resources, Committee on Government Reform, U.S. House of Representatives, July 13, 1999, at www.norml.org/recreational/testimony990.shtml (accessed October 12, 2001).

5. A counterargument holds that, given the rebellious streak of adolescents, legalizing marijuana for adolescents as well as adults might diminish the

drug's allure, thus reducing adolescent use. Whether this would actually be the case is difficult to ascertain.

6. William F. Buckley Jr., "The War on Drugs Is Lost," *National Review* 48 (February 12, 1996): 35–36.

7. Buckley, "War on Drugs Is Lost," 36–38.

8. Julie Sevrens Lyons and Lisa M. Krieger, "Million Dollar Questions: How to Begin, End Cycle of Addiction," *San Jose Mercury News*, May 8, 2001.

9. Leo E. Hollister and James T. McDonough Jr., "Marijuana," *Encyclopedia of Drugs, Alcohol, and Addictive Behavior*, 2:706.

10. "Is Marijuana a 'Gateway' Drug That Leads Users to Try More Dangerous Drugs Like Cocaine? Yes," *CQ Researcher* 5, no. 28 (July 28, 1995): 673. Critics of the Center on Addiction and Substance Abuse dismiss the center's statistics as faulty and of little significance. See, for example, John P. Morgan and Lynn Zimmer, "Is Marijuana a 'Gateway' Drug That Leads Users to Try More Dangerous Drugs Like Cocaine? No," *CQ Researcher* 5, no. 28 (July 28, 1995): 673.

11. *Marihuana: A Signal of Misunderstanding* (see n. 2).

12. *Marihuana: A Signal of Misunderstanding*.

13. Stephen Jay Gould, *The Mismeasure of Man* (New York: Norton, 1996), 242.

14. Quoted in "The Marijuana Debate Goes On," *CQ Researcher* 1, no. 43 (November 20, 1998): 1018.

15. See, for example, "Antisocial Youths Prone to Marijuana Addiction," *Chronicle of Higher Education*, April 24, 1998.

16. *Marihuana: A Signal of Misunderstanding*.

17. "Monkeys Seek Repeated Doses of Marijuana Ingredient in Experiment," *AP Worldstream*, October 15, 2000.

18. Quoted in "Monkeys Seek Repeated Doses of Marijuana Ingredient in Experiment."

19. Some insights might be gained by studying drug use patterns in a country such as the Netherlands, where recreational use of marijuana has been decriminalized. One study has been interpreted as showing that decriminalization of marijuana in the Netherlands has not led to increased drug use (Jennifer McNulty, "Dutch Drug Policies Do Not Increase Marijuana Use," *Cannabis News*, May 2, 2004, at www.cannabisnews.com/news/thread18782.shtml [accessed November 26, 2004]). However, as in the case of physician-assisted suicide, care must be taken so that too much is not read into the data. Because of cultural differences and other variables, one should not assume that the Netherlands experience would be replicated in the United States or in any other country.

Ten Questions for Reflection and Discussion

1 What, if anything, is wrong with recreational use of marijuana?

2 What might be done to discourage adolescents from using marijuana and other mind-altering drugs?

3 Is marijuana addictive?

4 Does the use of marijuana lead to the use of other drugs such as cocaine and heroin?

5 What are the social costs related to the recreational use of marijuana?

6 Are these costs acceptable or unacceptable?

7 What might be done to minimize social costs related to the use of marijuana?

8 Under what circumstances, if any, should the use of marijuana be prohibited?

9 Has the war on drugs failed?

10 What should the policy of colleges and universities be with respect to recreational use of marijuana by students, faculty, and staff?

4

ABORTION

—

Three decades have passed since the U.S. Supreme Court redefined the legal landscape by delivering the *Roe v. Wade* and *Doe v. Bolton* decisions.[1] The years, however, have in no way softened the intensity of the debate about abortion.

As all who have wrestled with this most difficult of all issues are keenly aware, the status of the fetus plays a crucial role in the debate. Is the fetus a living human being, the death of which is analogous to the loss of a son or daughter, a sister or a brother? Or is what dies when an abortion is performed the moral equivalent of the death of the tonsils when a tonsillectomy is performed or the appendix when an appendectomy is performed? Or is the fetus somewhere in between— something more than just living human tissue but something less than an individual human being in the full sense of the term?[2]

The significance of this question is readily apparent. There is broad consensus favoring intervention when what someone does threatens the lives, health, and well-being of others. But does the fetus count as a someone, as an individual human being whose well-being is threatened if a pregnant woman contemplates ending her pregnancy via abortion? Or is intervention in such situations unwarranted intrusion that violates a pregnant woman's right of privacy?

In *Roe v. Wade*, the Court ruled against intervention to prohibit abortion prior to the time of viability. Justice Harry Blackmun, who delivered the opinion of the Court in *Roe v. Wade*, acknowledged that the "Constitution does not explicitly mention any right of privacy" but that in numerous decisions, "the Court has recognized that a right of personal privacy, or a guarantee of certain areas or zones of privacy, does exist under the Constitution." He further stated, "This right of privacy, whether it be founded in the Fourteenth Amendment's concept of personal liberty and restrictions upon state action, as we feel it is, or, as the District Court determined, in the Ninth Amendment's reservation of rights to the people, is broad enough to encompass a woman's decision whether or not to terminate her pregnancy." This right, however, "is not unqualified and must be considered against important state interests in regulation." As for intervention to protect the fetus, Justice Blackmun argued that "the 'compelling' point is at viability. This is so because the fetus then presumably has the capability of meaningful life outside the mother's womb. . . . If the State is interested in protecting fetal life after viability, it may go so far as to proscribe abortion during that period, except when it is necessary to preserve the life or health of the mother." The Court defined *viability* as "potentially able to live outside the mother's womb, albeit with artificial aid," a definition reaffirmed three years later in *Planned Parenthood of Missouri v. Danforth*.[3]

But did the Court draw the line in the right place?

THREE SCHOOLS OF THOUGHT

There is a certain literal sense in which the flame of life is passed from cell to cell and from generation to generation in a continuous process. But even though the flame of life is passed from one candle to another, it still makes sense to ask when the flame on an individual candle first appears and begins to send forth light and when that flame dies out and no longer provides illumination. Thus, even though life is a continuous process, the question of when the life of an individual human being begins and when it ends is of moral and legal significance.

Sketched in somewhat general terms, there are three schools of thought with respect to when human life begins—that is, the life of a human being.[4] One school of thought, sometimes labeled the genetic school, holds that human life begins at the time of conception, when an egg and sperm unite combining their genetic material to form the genotype (genetic code) of a new strand of life. John T. Noonan Jr. states, "The positive argument for conception as the decisive moment of humanization is that at conception the new being receives the genetic code."[5] Elsewhere he has observed, "I myself know only one test for humanity: a being who was conceived by human parents and is potentially capable of human acts is human."[6] A recent statement on human embryonic stem cell research issued by the Pontifical Academy for Life asserts, "On the basis of a complete biological analysis, the living human embryo is—from the moment of the union of the gametes—a *human subject* with a well defined identity, which from that point begins its own *coordinated, continuous and gradual development*, such that at no later stage can it be considered as a simple mass of cells."[7]

At the other end of the spectrum is the tissue school, which holds that the fertilized egg and the embryo, at least in the early stages of development, are nothing more than living human tissue until some threshold is reached, after which an individual human being is present. Thomas A. Shannon and Allan B. Wolter observe, "We find it impossible to speak of a true individual, an ontological individual, as present from fertilization. There is a time period of about three weeks during which it is biologically unrealistic to speak of a physical individual. This means that the reality of a person, however one might define that term, is not present at least until individualization has occurred."[8] Roy U.

Schenk has argued, "Each human fetus progresses through a continuous series of developmental stages and ultimately passes through [the] level of complexity at which self-awareness becomes possible. It seems reasonable to propose that this is the point at which the fetus changes from a potential to an actual human being."[9] Mary Anne Warren argues that "women are already persons in the usual nonlegal sense—already thinking, self-aware, fully social beings—and fetuses are not." She concludes, "Even sentient fetuses do not yet have either the cognitive capacities or the richly interactive social involvements typical of persons."[10]

As these examples illustrate, those in the tissue school do not necessarily agree when in the developmental process the threshold is reached that marks the beginning of the life of an individual human being. Some would place this threshold relatively early in the pregnancy while others would place it relatively late in the pregnancy, perhaps not even until birth occurs. But regardless of where this threshold is placed, the common denominator of those in the tissue school is that before this threshold, all that is present is living human tissue but that once this threshold is passed, an individual human being is present.

Somewhere between the genetic school and the tissue school is the developmental school. Both the genetic and tissue schools view the beginning of human life as an all-or-nothing type of event, one that occurs in a relatively brief period. The developmental school takes a different approach, that of viewing the beginning of human life as a process that extends over a considerable period, perhaps even throughout the entire pregnancy. This school of thought views the fertilized egg as something more than mere living human tissue but something less than an individual human being. As the developmental process continues, more is present until finally a threshold is reached denoting the presence of a human being, in the full sense of the term. As in the case of the tissue school, there is no consensus about when in the developmental process this threshold is reached.

One variant of the developmental school views fetal development as a linear process, with each day bringing a greater measure of life. For example, a social statement on abortion adopted by the Evangelical Lutheran Church in America states, "Although abortion raises significant moral issues at any stage of fetal development, the closer the life in the womb comes to full term the more serious such issues become."[11]

Another variant of the developmental school views the morally significant aspects of fetal development as a stair-step process with various thresholds marking a progressively higher status for the fetus. Though the Supreme Court did not specifically have this typology in mind when deciding *Roe v. Wade*, a rough facsimile of the stair-step approach is reflected in the decision. Before viability, the fetus has limited rights, such as the right to inherit property or, in some cases, even the right to share proceeds of a trust fund.[12] As noted, the Court ruled that once viability is reached, states may, but need not, protect the fetus by prohibiting abortion except in cases in which continuing the pregnancy would endanger the life or health of the pregnant woman. Birth marks yet another step upward in the status of the fetus, for once birth occurs, the newborn infant receives the full protection of the law.[13]

THE LIVING TISSUE ARGUMENT

The inconvenient fact about beginning-of-life issues is that sooner or later, regardless of the position one might take, just about everyone ends up getting painted into a corner. Take, for example, the widely held view that a human life is present from the time of conception. Suppose that Jones, a forty-eight-year-old male, is on the waiting list for a heart transplant. Smith, a twenty-three-year-old male who didn't happen to be wearing a helmet while riding his motorcycle, suffers severe traumatic head injuries. When the ambulance arrives, he is not breathing and his heart has stopped beating. The emergency medical response team makes a valiant effort to resuscitate him, but to no avail. When the ambulance arrives at the nearest hospital trauma center, a physician on duty determines that continued efforts to resuscitate him are futile. Smith is carrying a signed organ-donor card. With his wife's permission and once death has been declared, his heart and other organs are removed for transplant. Jones receives Smith's heart. The transplant surgery is successful, and Jones recovers to resume an active life, once again playing tennis and doing everything else he did before heart disease curtailed his activity.

Cells with Smith's genotype form the heart that is beating away in Jones's body. Does this mean that Smith is still alive, even though a physician determined that he was no longer living and even though after his funeral, his mortal remains, minus the organs taken for transplant, were buried? Hardly. We would typically say that while Smith's heart is still alive, albeit in Jones's body, Smith himself is no longer alive.

But if Smith himself is no longer alive, notwithstanding the fact that cells with his genotype are still alive and well, what distinguishes this situation from that of a fertilized egg? To put this in slightly different words, if genetic identity determines the presence of human life, why wouldn't someone of the genetic school—which says that human life begins at the time of conception—say that Smith is still alive as long as his heart keeps beating away in Jones's body?

There are two possible responses to this conundrum. One is to make a "whole organism" argument by saying that the fertilized egg represents a whole organism whereas Smith's heart, beating away in Jones's body, is simply an organ that is part of an organism. This response, however, gets the genetic school proponent painted into a corner rather quickly. If something needs to be a whole organism to be a someone, does this mean that those without tonsils or appendixes are no longer alive? That would undoubtedly come as quite a surprise to those who have undergone tonsillectomies or appendectomies! At this point in the discussion, the genetic school proponent typically responds by saying that some organs and functions are essential whereas others, such as the tonsils and the appendix, are not. This response, however, implicitly abandons the claim that human life begins at the time of conception. If certain key biological functions are necessary for human life to be present, then genetic identity alone does not make something a someone.

There is a second response the genetic school proponent can make to the living tissue argument, one that doesn't get the proponent painted into a corner quite as quickly as the whole organism response. The genetic school proponent can respond by saying that the fertilized egg has the potential of becoming a fully developed human being whereas Smith's heart, beating away in Jones's body, does not. But once again, the genetic school proponent has abandoned the contention that human life begins at the time of conception. If the fertilized egg should be treated as if it were a human being because it has the potential of becoming a fully developed human being, then it is by definition not an actual human being. Potentiality is not actuality.

VALUING POTENTIAL HUMAN LIFE

The potentiality response to the living tissue argument, however, does raise an important question: how should potential human life be viewed and valued? Should potential human life be accorded the same value as actual human life (as the second genetic school response to the living tissue argument suggests)? Or should potential human life be accorded no value at all, other than whatever value it possesses as living human tissue? Or is the moral significance of potential human life something somewhere betwixt and between?

In an article published several years ago, Edward Langerak argues that something betwixt and between is the best way to view potential human life. He states, "The potentiality principle asks us to respect a potential person by virtue not of what it *could* be, but of what it *will* be in the normal course of its development." To illustrate the point, he uses the analogy of a president-elect, whom he labels a "potential president." He states, "The person is not yet commander-in-chief but, in the normal course, *will* (not *could*) be. Already that person receives some of the perquisites of the future office."[14]

As Langerak correctly notes, we typically view a president-elect as more important than a candidate for election or anyone else who is a possible president but not with the same degree of respect and importance as an actual president. In effect, eggs and sperm are like candidates for president, the majority of whom do not end up being presidents. But once the election is held, the odds of becoming president increase greatly for the candidate who received a majority of the electoral votes. Similarly, once fertilization occurs, the odds that an egg and a sperm will become a fully developed human being increase greatly. In both cases, the potentiality will be realized, barring unforeseen circumstances such as unexpected death. But just as a president-elect is not yet a president, so also is the developing embryo not yet a person, in the full sense of the term. It is a potential person, just as the president-elect is a potential president. And just as a president-elect is accorded greater value and respect than a presidential candidate but not as much as an actual president, so also ought the developing embryo be accorded greater value and respect than eggs and sperm but not as much as an actual human being.

AN ARGUMENT BASED ON CONSISTENCY

Langerak's argument makes a good deal of sense. The task of drawing lines, however, still remains. We know when a president-elect becomes an actual president: the oath of office during the inaugural ceremony marks the transfer of power from the old president to the new president. What line or lines of demarcation, however, mark the transition from potential human life to actual human life?

One of the ironies of modern technology is that formerly simple matters have now become exceedingly complex. This is true with respect to not only abortion but other areas as well. Before the advent of modern medicine, there was little doubt about when people died: when they stopped breathing and their hearts stopped beating, they were no longer alive. But with the advent of life-support systems and organ donation, many in the medical community and elsewhere perceived a need for updated guidelines for determining when death has occurred. Responding to this concern in the early 1980s, the President's Commission for the Study of Ethical Problems in Medicine and Biomedical and Behavioral Research proposed a Uniform Determination of Death Act:

> An individual who has sustained either (1) irreversible cessation of circulatory and respiratory functions, or (2) irreversible cessation of all functions of the entire brain, including the brain stem, is dead. A determination of death must be made in accordance with accepted medical standards.[15]

The commission noted that it would be "conceptually acceptable" to follow the lead of a Canadian law reform commission in proposing "the irreversible cessation of brain functions as *the* 'definition' and then to permit that standard to be met not only by direct measures of brain activity but also 'by the prolonged absence of spontaneous cardiac and respiratory functions.'" The commission concluded, however, that such an approach would be an unnecessary break with tradition, noting that "for most lay people—and in all probability for most physicians as well—the permanent loss of heart and lung function . . . clearly manifests death."[16] Thus, while the proposed guidelines suggest a dual track for determining death, the emphasis is on irreversible cessation of all brain activity, including that of the brain stem.

The Uniform Determination of Death Act has gained wide acceptance. Thirty-one states, the District of Columbia, and the U.S. Virgin

Islands have adopted the statute as proposed. Other states have incorporated the proposed guidelines in other laws.[17]

What does this have to do with the beginning of life? If a particular set of guidelines determines when a human being is no longer alive, then there is an argument based on consistency for using the same guidelines to determine when a human being first becomes alive. Unless there are compelling reasons for using different standards for determining the beginning and end of one's life, there is much to be said for consistency.

If a case is to be made for applying the Uniform Determination of Death Act guidelines to the beginning of life, two basic issues must be addressed:

- Is the concept of human life implicit in the proposed Uniform Determination of Death Act defensible? Or is there some other, preferable understanding of what it is that makes something a someone?

- Does it make sense to apply the brain activity guideline to the beginning of life? Or are there compelling reasons for asymmetry— that is, for using one set of guidelines to determine when life begins and a different set of guidelines for determining when life ends?

WHAT IS IT THAT MAKES SOMETHING A SOMEONE?

In the final analysis, the question of when life begins and when life ends is not a biological question. The presence of *Homo sapiens* brain activity is of moral significance only if one assumes that brain activity is both a necessary and a sufficient condition for something to be a someone. That assumption, however, rests on some very basic notions about what it is to be a person. (For purposes of this discussion, I am using the terms *person, human being,* and *individual human life* interchangeably.) If one assumes that having a unique human genotype or being able to breathe spontaneously is a necessary and sufficient condition for something to be a someone, then what those in the life sciences can tell us about the functioning of the brain, while interesting, is not of moral significance. In short, the operative value presuppositions are what determine the moral significance of various biological functions.

I shall not attempt to summarize centuries of speculation about what it is that makes something a someone. It does seem to me, however, that the philosophers and theologians who speak of "conscious being in the world" or "embodied consciousness" are pointing in the right direction. Succinctly stated, being human involves being aware of what is happening on at least some level. Social interaction is also important.

The consciousness that enables awareness and social interaction, however, does not float unattached throughout all time and all places. We cannot be someone else, live in some other era, or be in more than one place simultaneously. Consciousness is fixed in both time and place by the biological substrata that make it possible. When these basic biological functions are not yet present or no longer present, consciousness is not possible. Robert M. Veatch states, "What is critical is the embodied capacity for consciousness or social interaction. When this embodied capacity is gone, I am gone. When there is no longer any capacity for consciousness, to think and feel within a human body, then I am gone."[18]

The foregoing suggests that the portions of the brain related to consciousness serve as the key biological functions for determining whether the life of a human being is present. And indeed there is a case to be made for using higher brain function as the indicator of human life and its irreversible loss as indication that a person is no longer living. For a number of years, Veatch has been in the forefront of those arguing the case for this approach. In a book first published in 1976 that continues to be an important reference point in the debate, Veatch states,

Determining the locus of consciousness and social interaction certainly requires greater scientific understanding, but evidence points strongly to the neocortex or outer surface of the brain as the site. Indeed, if this is the locus of consciousness, the presence or absence of activity in the rest of the brain will be immaterial to the holder of this view.[19]

But many find a higher brain definition of death outside their comfort zone. If an individual is declared dead on the basis of a higher brain definition of death yet still has a functioning brain stem, it is biologically possible for that individual to still be breathing spontaneously. And in some cases, with a little assistance, that individual could even walk to the morgue. The President's Commission suggests that it is problematic that "patients in whom only the neocortex or subcortical areas have been damaged may still retain or regain spontaneous respiration and circulation." They note that the implication of higher brain formulations is that, according to such a guideline, an individual who has suffered irreversible loss of higher brain function "is just as dead as a corpse in the traditional sense," even though spontaneous respiration continues. "The Commission rejects this conclusion and the further implication that such patients could be buried or otherwise treated as dead persons."[20]

For some, discomfort with sending spontaneously breathing bodies to the morgue might be the result of projecting consciousness onto whatever is there, even though there is no biological or psychological evidence indicating that consciousness is possible once higher brain functions are irretrievably lost. Others find a higher brain guideline unacceptable because they prefer a broader guideline. James L. Bernat writes, "Once we accept the definition of death as the permanent cessation of critical functions of the organism as a whole, the next task is to identify the criterion that shows that this definition has been fulfilled. . . . The criterion of death that best fulfills this function is the irreversible cessation of all clinical functions of the brain."[21]

There is a strong case to be made for suggesting that the end of life, like the beginning of life, is a process that extends over a considerable period, rather than an event that occurs in a limited period. Referring to the biological functions that phase out at various points in the dying process, Baruch A. Brody suggests that it is "reasonable to say that the organism was fully alive before the chain of events began, is fully dead by the end of the chain of events, and is neither during the process."[22]

That might be true from a biological perspective, but a line needs to be drawn somewhere for a host of practical reasons, ranging from organ donation to insurance and other matters. The whole-brain guideline provides a plausible and practical way to draw the line.

ARE THERE COMPELLING REASONS FOR ASYMMETRY?

Quite obviously, there are differences between the beginning of life and the end of life. But are these morally significant differences—differences that would warrant using one set of guidelines to determine when human life begins and another for determining when it ends?

One obvious difference is that the fertilized egg has the potential of becoming a fully developed human being, if all goes well, whereas the mortal remains of someone who has been declared dead on the basis of the whole-brain guideline do not. But as already noted, potentiality is not the same as actuality. While there is a case to be made for according potential human life greater value than, say, a tonsil or other living human tissue, to view potential human life as morally indistinguishable from actual human life is a stretch. Moreover, even if one does conclude that potential human life ought to be accorded the same value as actual human life, such a conclusion does not substantiate a claim that individual human life begins before the presence of brain activity. It merely suggests that whatever is there before brain activity ought to be treated as if it were a human life.

Another obvious difference between the beginning of life and the end of life is that death marks the end of the life of a person who has existed within a web of social relationships, whereas the embryo has not experienced social relationships, at least not to the same extent. But does being a person—or somewhat more specifically, being a living human being—depend on social perceptions, on being known by others? Does lack of mourners at someone's funeral mean that death occurred long ago, if indeed that person ever was alive? Hardly. Moreover, to say that once birth occurs, individuals live in a web of social relationships, whereas the fetuses do not, might not accurately reflect all prenatal situations. We all know prospective parents who have chosen the name of the child yet to be born, who sing or play music for the fetus *in utero* and treat the fetus as if he or she is already a member of the family.

Some resistance to the notion of using a brain activity standard to denote the beginning of human life will undoubtedly come from proponents of abortion who want to make abortion as easy as possible and who want to justify it as late in the pregnancy as possible. But is this not a case of arguing from conclusions to premises, of deciding where one wants to come out on the issue of abortion and then hunting for presuppositions to support these conclusions? Sometimes what we want to conclude is at odds with rules of logic. Is there not something to be said for accepting conclusions derived from defensible premises rather than starting with the conclusions we hope to reach and then looking around for premises to support them?

As for symmetry versus asymmetry, D. Gareth Jones argues, "Definitions of death apply specifically to those who are dying, not to those who are developing. Development and degeneration are not interchangeable."[23] He is, of course, at least partially right about that. Development and degeneration are not the same thing. However, it is not the guidelines per se that are the key consideration but rather the concept of person that underlies them (i.e., what it is that defines a human life). An argument based on consistency holds that the same concept of person ought to be used to determine both the beginning and the end of an individual human life.[24]

When all things are considered, I can find no compelling reasons for using a double standard for determining when human life begins and ends. All that remains is to determine the line marking the beginning of human life.

The brain function guideline proposed by the President's Commission asserts that as long as any brain function whatsoever is present, including that of the brain stem, a person is still alive, even if some brain functions are irretrievably lost. Applying the brain function guideline to the developing fetus means that an individual human life is present whenever brain function of any sort, including that of the brain stem, is first discernible. This threshold is reached somewhere around the eighth week of pregnancy.[25] Both conceptually and practically, drawing the line here makes a good deal of sense.

ROE V. WADE REVISITED

Applying a brain function guideline to the beginning of human life entails specifying a starting point earlier than that implied by the U.S. Supreme Court, when it stated that nontherapeutic abortions may, but need not, be prohibited once viability is reached but that such abortions could not be prohibited before that time.[26] Thus *Roe v. Wade* would either have to be reversed by the Court, which is unlikely, or revised by constitutional amendment, which, though not easy, is not impossible. A clarifying amendment would best serve its purposes if it specified who counts as a person with rights and liberties such as those specified by the Fourteenth Amendment. A constitutional amendment

CHAPTER 4

specifying when life begins and when life ends might be stated as follows:

> For purposes of this document, a person, with all of the rights and privileges guaranteed by this constitution as amended, shall be defined as an individual human being with the beginning of that individual's life denoted by the beginning of any form of brain activity, including that of the brain stem, and with the end of that individual's life denoted by irreversible cessation of all functions of that individual's brain, including the brain stem. This amendment shall not be construed as precluding abortions necessary to preserve the life of a pregnant woman.

Late-term abortions to save the life of the pregnant woman would in effect be sacrificing one life, that of the fetus, to save the life of another person. Sacrificing one life to save another life is invariably a morally anguishing decision. But it is the lesser of evils in some circumstances, particularly in view of the fact that failure to induce an abortion might result in the loss of two lives—the life of the fetus as well as the life of the pregnant woman. As James M. Gustafson put it in an essay published before *Roe v. Wade*, "As the morally conscientious soldier fighting in a particular war is convinced that life can and ought to be taken, 'justly' but also 'mournfully,' so the moralist can be convinced that the life of the defenseless fetus can be taken, less justly, but more mournfully."[27]

EARLY-TERM ABORTIONS

And what of abortions early in the pregnancy before the beginning of brain stem activity? As noted, it is plausible to view potential human life as having greater moral significance than living human tissue but not the same level of moral significance as actual human life. Such being the case, abortions early in the pregnancy do not require justifying reasons as weighty as those required for abortions once brain activity is detectable.

52

It is a close call as to which is preferable: specifying in law justifiable reasons for abortions early in the pregnancy, as several states attempted to do prior to *Roe v. Wade* and *Doe v. Bolton*;[28] or leaving this matter to the discretion of the pregnant woman. I am inclined toward the latter. I acknowledge that this approach would not preclude abortions for casual reasons. However, this risk—if indeed it exists—is likely to be less onerous than the endless litigation and legal hairsplitting that would inevitably accompany any return to specifying in law what counts as an acceptable reason for early-term abortions and what does not.

WHY INTERVENTION?

The foregoing clearly points in the direction of intervention to prevent most abortions once discernible fetal brain activity is present. But why intervene? Why not take a libertarian approach? Why not say, "Personally, I believe that abortion is wrong, but I have no business attempting to impose my views on other people"?

Toleration has limits. Suppose, for example, that a religious community inspired by the beliefs and practices of pre-Columbian Aztecs were to take root in this country and that these beliefs and practices included human sacrifice. Would anyone with deep moral reservations about human sacrifice (which I certainly have!) be likely to say, "Personally, I believe that human sacrifice is wrong, but I respect the right of others to practice their religion as they see fit"? No way. Freedom of religion as we understand and affirm it does not extend to killing other people. Nor does a right to privacy extend to killing other people, even though so doing might in some cases be convenient.

Standing with fetuses to protect them from whatever harm might befall them, however, is at best an incomplete response. Regrettably, some who speak out vociferously about the rights of a child yet to be born are nowhere to be found after the birth of that child when the time comes to care for that child and provide him or her with a nurturing environment. If one is to intervene to protect the rights of children yet to be born, there is also an obligation to make certain that child care programs are adequately funded and that the nutritional and other needs of children are satisfied. I am dismayed by the frequency with which those who strongly oppose abortion also strongly oppose providing adequate public funding for child nutrition programs and other programs intended to respond to the needs of disadvantaged children. There is an argument based on consistency to be made here as well.

As Mary Anne Warren correctly notes, many tests for fetal abnormalities, such as Down's syndrome and spina bifida, cannot be performed until the latter part of the second trimester. She writes, "The elimination of most such abortions might be a consequence that could be accepted, were the society willing to provide adequate support for the handicapped children and adults who would come into being as a result of this policy. However, our society is not prepared to do this."[29] The bottom line is that we had better get prepared to provide adequate support for handicapped children born as a result of more stringent abortion policies. To fail to do so would be unconscionable.

I am also dismayed by the harsh words of condemnation some opponents of abortion hurl at women contemplating abortion. If more compassion and understanding were extended, if there were greater willingness to respond to the needs and concerns of those experiencing unwanted pregnancies, any inclination to end the pregnancy by abortion might be diminished substantially. And when pregnant women choose to share their children with childless couples desperately hoping to become parents via adoption, those who make these courageous decisions need and deserve far more affirmation than they typically receive.[30] How many churches, for example, have liturgies of affirmation, be they public or private, for birth mothers who choose to entrust the lives of their children to adoptive parents and experience the anguish that often accompanies such decisions? We would all do well to be quicker to understand and slower to condemn.

SOME CONCLUDING CONSIDERATIONS

But while greater measures of compassion and understanding are desperately needed, that in no way obviates the fact that if we conclude that human life is present once brain activity is present, such a conclusion legislates strongly in favor of intervention to protect the fetus. In short, there is just cause for intervention.

But what of right intent, last resort, lawful authority, reasonable hope of success, and due proportionality? To be morally acceptable, any intervention to protect the brain-active fetus must be motivated by concern for the well-being of that fetus. Not to win votes in an election. Not for any reason other than concern for the well-being of the brain-active fetus.

Moreover, all efforts to curtail abortion must go through appropriate legal channels. The ethic of intervention being mapped out here does not allow vigilante action. It does not allow disrupting abortion clinics or threatening harm to those who perform abortions.

As for reasonable hope of success, here matters become more complicated. Would a more restrictive approach to abortion reduce the number of brain-active fetuses aborted? Probably, though some abortions of brain-active fetuses would undoubtedly continue. But saving some lives is surely preferable to saving none at all.

But what about due proportionality? Would more restrictive abortion laws simply push women with unwanted pregnancies into the hands of unscrupulous back-alley abortionists, providing fertile ground for organized crime to flourish in a replay of what happened when efforts were made to prohibit the consumption of alcoholic beverages?

That could happen. This possibility is the strongest argument for maintaining *Roe v. Wade* in its present form.

Such an outcome, however, is by no means a foregone conclusion. If we are willing to move away from narrowly defined preconceptions, if we are willing to look beyond our immediate concerns and agendas, and if we are willing to take a fresh look at the issues related to abortion—including the status of the brain-active fetus and the ways of reaching out to and being understanding of women with unwanted pregnancies—a new era of hope and affirmation are possible.

Traditional just war theory holds that military intervention should always be done reluctantly and with regret. The same is true to an even greater extent with respect to abortion. With this reluctance and regret should come not only affirmation of the personhood and well-being of the brain-active fetus but, in equal measure, affirmation of the personhood and well-being of those experiencing unwanted pregnancies.

NOTES

1. In *Roe v. Wade* (410 U.S. 113), the Court struck down a Texas law prohibiting all abortions except those necessary to save the life of a pregnant woman. In *Doe v. Bolton* (410 U.S. 179), the Court reviewed a Georgia law. Georgia had revised its abortion law to allow abortion if continuing the pregnancy would endanger the pregnant woman's life or health, if there was a high probability the fetus would be born with a serious defect, or if the pregnancy resulted from rape. The Court ruled that the Georgia law was unconstitutional. When the Court rules a law in one state unconstitutional, similar laws in other states are also struck down; thus, the practical impact of *Roe v. Wade* and *Doe v. Bolton* was that abortion laws in all but four states were wiped off the books. The only exceptions were Alaska, Hawaii, New York, and Washington, which had passed repeal laws allowing abortion upon request to state residents, subject to certain time limitations and procedural requirements. Because the time parameters specified by the four states did not coincide with those specified by the Court in *Roe v. Wade*, the Alaska, Hawaii, New York, and

Washington laws had to undergo some revision in the wake of *Roe v. Wade*. For an overview of the history of abortion laws in the United States prior to *Roe v. Wade* and *Doe v. Bolton*, see Betty Sarvis and Hyman Rodman, *The Abortion Controversy*, 2nd ed. (New York: Columbia University Press, 1974), 27–68. For an overview of federal abortion policies in the United states after *Roe v. Wade* and *Doe v. Bolton*, see Brian L. Wilcox, Jennifer K. Robbennolt, and Janet E. O'Keeffe, "Federal Abortion Policy and Politics: 1973 to 1996," in *The New Civil War: The Psychology, Culture, and Politics of Abortion*, ed. Linda J. Beckman and S. Marie Harvey (Washington, D.C.: American Psychological Association, 1998), 3–24.

2. While the conclusion one reaches about the status of the fetus defines an important part of the landscape with respect to the debate about abortion, the status of the fetus does not absolutely determine where one will come out with respect to the morality of abortion. It is possible to oppose abortion without arguing that the fetus represents a human life, by insisting, for example, that there is a sanctity to the process of human procreation and any intervention in this process is illicit. Similarly, it is possible to believe that the fetus is a human being and make a case for abortion, though this necessitates arguing that sacrificing the life of the fetus is justifiable under some circumstances. In a widely reprinted article, Judith Jarvis Thomson makes precisely this type of argument ("On the Moral and Legal Status of Abortion," *Philosophy and Public Affairs* 1, no. 1 [Fall 1971]: 47–66). At the end of the article, she notes, "At this place, however, it should be remembered that we have only been pretending throughout that the fetus is a human being from the moment of conception. A very early abortion is surely not the killing of a person, and so is not dealt with by anything I have said here." For an engaging discussion of Thomson's argument, see F. M. Kamm, *Creation and Abortion: A Study in Moral and Legal Philosophy* (New York: Oxford University Press, 1992), 20, 72–76.

3. *Planned Parenthood of Missouri v. Danforth*, 428 U.S. 52 (1976). Justice Harry Blackmun, who delivered the opinion of the Court, stated, "In Roe, we used the term 'viable,' properly we thought, to signify the point at which the fetus is 'potentially able to live outside the mother's womb, albeit with artificial aid,' and presumably capable of 'meaningful life outside the mother's womb.'"

4. The typology used here is a variation of one sketched out by Daniel Callahan in *Abortion: Law, Choice, and Morality* (New York: Macmillan, 1970), 378–404. Callahan labels the three schools of thought "the genetic school,"

"the developmental school," and the "social consequences school." The social consequences school, as Callahan defines it, holds that any decision with respect to when human life begins should be made on the basis of the social consequences of that decision. Strictly speaking, however, that is not a view with respect to when human life begins but rather a method of decision making. The developmental school, as Callahan uses the term, does not distinguish between those who believe that the fetus is nothing more than living human tissue before some point in the developmental process and those who believe that the beginning of human life is an incremental process. To distinguish these fundamentally different views, I reserve the use of the developmental school label for the latter view while referring to those who view the fetus as nothing more than human tissue before some point in the developmental process as members of the tissue school.

5. John T. Noonan Jr., "An Almost Absolute Value in History," in *The Morality of Abortion: Legal and Historical Perspectives*, ed. John T. Noonan Jr. (Cambridge, Mass.: Harvard University Press, 1970), 57.

6. Quoted by Callahan in *Abortion*, 379.

7. Pontifical Academy for Life, "Declaration on the Production and the Scientific and Therapeutic Use of Human Embryonic Stem Cells," at http://authors.va.mondosearch.com/cgi-bin/MsmGo.exe?grab_id=64541334&EXTRA_ARG=&CFGNAME=MssFind%2Ecfg&host_id=1&page_id=2851&query=Stem+Cell+Research&hiword=STEM+CELL+RESEARCH+> (accessed May 10, 2002).

8. Thomas A. Shannon and Allan B. Wolter, "Reflections on the Moral Status of the Pre-embryo," in *Bioethics*, 4th ed., ed. Thomas A. Shannon (Mahwah, N.J.: Paulist Press, 1993), 53. A case can also be made for placing Shannon and Walter in the developmental school.

9. Quoted by Callahan in *Abortion*, 385.

10. Mary Anne Warren, "The Moral Significance of Birth," in *Bioethics, Justice, and Health Care*, ed. Wanda Teays and Laura M. Purdy (Belmont, Calif.: Wadsworth / Thomson Learning, 2001), 480.

11. Evangelical Lutheran Church in America, *A Social Statement on Abortion*, www.elca.org/dcs/abortion.html (accessed May 12, 2002).

12. *Roe v. Wade* did not overturn *Industrial Trust Co. v. Wilson*, 61 R.I. 169, 200 A. 467 (1938). In this case, the Supreme Court of Rhode Island ruled that Melba Colt, who was born after the death of her father, should receive a portion of the income of a trust fund starting at the date of the death

of her father rather than the date of her birth. Thus, in effect, she received income *in utero*, though, of course, actual payment was not made until some time later.

13. In many discussions of abortion, the question of whether the fetus represents a human life tends to get intertwined with the question of whether the fetus has any rights. Granted, in many cases, questions of human life and questions of human rights are different ways of addressing the same issue. However, the assumption that when human life is present, human rights are present and vice versa is not always consistent with rights claims that are made. Take, for example, the assertion that we ought to be concerned about the rights of future generations and, accordingly, ought not deplete the topsoil of productive farmland or contaminate groundwater with cancer-causing chemicals. Those who will constitute future generations have not yet been born. So in this case, at least, there are rights claims that pertain to people who do not yet exist. It can also go the other way. Those who defend capital punishment in effect say that there is at least one basic human right—the right to continued existence, or, if you prefer, the right to life—that does not pertain to the convicted murderer on death row. Thus, at least in the eyes of those who defend capital punishment (many of whom also oppose abortion), the right to life is not necessarily coextensive with the existence of human life. Insofar as the status of the fetus is concerned, however, the distinction between the presence of human life and the presence of human rights is one that for the most part does not need to be made.

14. Edward Langerak, "Abortion: Listening to the Middle," *Hastings Center Report* 9, no. 5 (October 1979): 25–26.

15. President's Commission for the Study of Ethical Problems in Medicine and Biomedical and Behavioral Research, *Defining Death: Medical, Legal, and Ethical Issues in the Determination of Death* (Washington, D.C.: U.S. Government Printing Office, 1981), 2.

16. President's Commission, *Defining Death*, 74.

17. Alexander Morgan Capron, "The Bifurcated Legal Standard for Determining Death: Does It Work?" in *The Definition of Death: Contemporary Controversies*, ed. Stuart J. Youngner, Robert M. Arnold, and Renie Schapiro (Baltimore: Johns Hopkins University Press, 1999), 117, 133–44. Capron served as executive director for the President's Commission for the Study of Ethical Problems in Medicine and Biomedical and Behavioral Research while the commission was preparing the report on defining death.

18. Robert M. Veatch, "Whole-Brain, Neocortical, and Higher Brain Related Concepts," in *Death: Beyond Whole-Brain Criteria*, ed. Richard M. Zaner (Dordrecht, Holland: Kluwer Academic Publishers, 1988), 182. Veatch explains, "I, like a great many in our society, stand in the Judeo-Christian tradition. As such I maintain two things. First, I maintain that the human is fundamentally a social animal, a member of a human community capable of interacting with other humans. Second, I maintain that I am in essence the conjoining of soul and body—or to use the more modern language, mind and body."

19. Robert M. Veatch, *Death, Dying, and the Biological Revolution: Our Last Quest for Responsibility* (New Haven, Conn.: Yale University Press, 1976), 45. In the revised edition published by Yale University Press in 1989, Veatch acknowledges that there is uncertainty as to exactly which portions of the brain are related to consciousness. He notes that because of this uncertainty, he prefers "purposely to speak more vaguely of a 'higher brain' locus of this concept of death rather than being overly concrete in using terms such as 'cerebral,' 'cortical,' or 'neocortical'" (34). Veatch has also written several articles on the subject, including "The Whole-Brain-Oriented Concept of Death: An Outmoded Philosophical Formulation," *Journal of Thanatology* 3, no. 1 (1975): 13–30; "The Impending Collapse of the Whole-Brain Definition of Death," *Hastings Center Report* 23, no. 4 (July/August 1993): 18–24; and "Brain Death and Slippery Slopes," *Journal of Clinical Ethics* 3 (1992): 181–87. Veatch makes a distinction between "personhood" and a "living human being." In "The Impending Collapse," he states, "I, for one, have acknowledged the possibility that there are living human beings who do not satisfy the various concepts of personhood. As long as the law is only discussing whether someone is a living individual, the debate over personhood is irrelevant" (20). In "Brain Death and Slippery Slopes," Veatch suggests that it is not a foregone conclusion that a higher-brain definition of death is a new definition. He states, "A higher-brain-oriented definition of death is any of a number of definitions that reflect the concept of death as irreversible loss of all mental or 'higher' functions. It is not obvious that this differs significantly from traditional concepts of death, especially those of the Judeo-Christian tradition that emphasized that a human entity is one who necessarily involves the integration of body, spirit, and soul" (182).

20. President's Commission, *Defining Death*, 40.

21. James L. Bernat, "A Defense of the Whole-Brain Concept of Death," *Hastings Center Report* 28, no. 2 (March/April 1998): 14–24.

22. Baruch A. Brody, "How Much of the Brain Must Be Dead?" in Youngner, Arnold, and Schapiro, *The Definition of Death*, 79.

23. D. Gareth Jones, "The Problematic Symmetry between Brain Birth and Brain Death," *Journal of Medical Ethics* 24 (August 1998): 243. See also J. M. Goldenring, "The Brain-Life Theory: Toward a Consistent Biological Definition of Humanness," *Journal of Medical Ethics* 11 (1985): 198–204; and D. Gareth Jones, "Brain Birth and Personal Identity," *Journal of Medical Ethics* 15 (1989): 173–78.

24. Jones notes that among those who wish to use a brain-function reference point to determine when human life begins, there is a range of opinion about how much central nervous system activity is necessary before it makes sense to say that a human life is present. And indeed, various facets of the central nervous system develop over a considerable period that encompasses almost all of the pregnancy. Jones concludes, "Such a vast time period is too crude to prove convincing embryologically, and is too diffuse to prove helpful ethically ("The Problematic Symmetry between Brain Birth and Brain Death," 242). The problem, however, is not any different from that encountered when trying to determining when the life of an individual human being has ended, particularly in cases in which the degenerative process stretches out over a considerable period. But it is conceptually possible and practically necessary to come to at least some sort of conclusion about where the line should be, as did the President's Commission in proposing the Uniform Determination of Death Act. Should not the concept of what it is to be a person that informed the President's Commission's proposal also be used to determine when the life of an individual human being begins? Granted, there is controversy in both cases regarding exactly where the line should be drawn. But does controversy obviate the need to draw the line somewhere? And does such controversy in any way invalidate the consistency argument?

25. For a detailed discussion of the development of the human central nervous system, see Keith L. Moore and T. V. N. Persaud, *The Developing Human: Clinically Oriented Embryology*, 6th ed. (Philadelphia: W. B. Saunders, 1998), 451–90. See also Ronald Munson, *Intervention and Reflection: Basic Issues in Medical Ethics*, 6th ed. (Belmont, Calif.: Wadsworth / Thomson Learning, 2000), 77–78. The end of the eighth week marks the end of the embryonic period and the beginning of the fetal period. By the end of the embryonic period, all of the major organ systems are in place, and all that remains is differentiation and growth of organs and tissue formed during the embryonic period.

26. The fact that the beginning of brain activity cannot always be determined with absolute precision does not invalidate the brain activity guideline. The point at which viability is first present is also difficult to determine—perhaps even more difficult than determining the beginning of brain activity since there are no tests comparable to an electroencephalogram (EEG) that can be used to measure viability. Yet, the Supreme Court saw no impropriety in using a viability reference point to determine how early in the pregnancy nontherapeutic abortions can be prohibited.

27. James M. Gustafson, "A Protestant Ethical Approach," in *The Morality of Abortion: Legal and Historical Perspectives*, ed. John T. Noonan Jr. (Cambridge, Mass.: Harvard University Press, 1970), 122.

28. Many of the states that passed modified abortion laws in the late 1960s followed, with some variation, the abortion law proposed by the American Law Institute in the model penal code released in 1962: "A licensed physician is justified in terminating a pregnancy if he believes there is a substantial risk that continuance of the pregnancy would gravely impair the physical or mental health of the mother, or that the child would be born with grave physical or mental defect, or that the pregnancy resulted from rape, incest, or other felonious intercourse." For a list of states that passed laws that incorporated this recommendation, in whole or in part, see Sarvis and Rodman, *Abortion Controversy*, 30–33.

29. Warren, "Moral Significance of Birth," 479.

30. I am greatly dismayed when I hear the phrase "give up for adoption." In the majority of cases in which birth mothers make the anguishing decision to share the life of their children with adoptive parents, they are not abandoning or giving away their children. Rather, the decision to share the life of the child via adoption is almost always a loving, caring decision that is motivated by a desire to do what is best for the child.

Ten Questions for Reflection and Discussion

1 What makes something a someone?

2 How early in the developmental process is it meaningful to speak of the life of an individual human being?

3 Under what circumstances, if any, is abortion justifiable?

4 Did the U.S. Supreme Court draw the line in the right place in *Roe v. Wade*?

5 When, if at all, should abortion be prohibited by law?

6 How, if at all, should *Roe v. Wade* be modified?

7 What might be done to help women deal with the trauma of unwanted pregnancies?

8 What might be done to help families of children with birth defects?

9 What might be done to be more affirmative and supportive of birth mothers who choose to share via adoption the lives of their children with couples and others wishing to be parents?

10 What might be done to diminish the harshness of the debate about abortion, thereby ensuring a greater degree of civility?

5

PARENTAL REFUSAL OF BENEFICIAL

MEDICAL TREATMENT FOR THEIR CHILDREN

—

Among the most anguishing situations are those in which well-meaning, loving parents either do not seek out medically beneficial treatment for their children or refuse to give their permission for this treatment. In some cases, such as blood transfusions for Jehovah's Witnesses and various forms of medical treatment for those who are Christian Scientists, the refusal stems from religious beliefs that differ from those held by most health care providers. In other cases, the refusal stems from assessments of risk and benefit that differ from prevailing views in the medical community.

At the outset, it should be noted that these cases should not simply be lumped together with child abuse cases in which indifferent or hostile parents neglect or deliberately harm their children. What distinguishes the type of cases noted here from cases of child abuse involving neglect or deliberate harm is that parents in the former cases care very much about the well-being of their children. But for various reasons, be they religious or secular, these well-meaning parents object to medically beneficial treatment because they do not view the treatment as appropriate for their children. When hostile or indifferent parents harm their children by physically injuring them or by failing to provide for physical needs such as nutrition, the case for intervention is relatively easy to make. But when loving, caring, well-meaning parents choose not to seek treatment that the medical community views as beneficial or when they refuse permission for this treatment, the case for intervention is far more difficult. Four sad and tragic cases illustrate what is at stake in these situations.

CASE A: AN ATTEMPT TO HEAL BY PRAYER

Eleven-year-old Ian Lundman, who had been intermittently ill and lethargic for several weeks, reported to his mother, Kathleen McKown, that he had a stomachache and did not feel well. Noting that her son had lost weight, had a fruity aroma on his breath, and lacked his normal level of energy, McKown, a devout Christian Scientist, began treating him through prayer. The next morning, when Ian again complained that he did not feel well, his mother's concern intensified. The Christian Science Church recommends that when a parent is concerned about the health of a child, a journal-listed Christian Science practitioner be contacted. (A Christian Science publication provides a list of those who have been trained to provide spiritual treatment through prayer.) McKown contacted Mario Tosto, a journal-listed practitioner, and hired him to pray for Ian. Throughout the day, Ian's condition continued to worsen.[1]

The next day, with Ian's condition continuing to deteriorate, his concerned mother and stepfather (also a Christian Scientist) sought additional help. Ian's mother, in keeping with directives issued by the church, contacted a church official. He verified that a journal-listed practitioner was involved in the case and notified the First Church of Christ Scientist in Boston (the "mother church" of Christian Science) that the child of a Christian Scientist was seriously ill. Ian's mother also contacted Clifton House, a Christian Science nursing home located in Minneapolis; a nurse there advised her to give Ian small quantities of liquids. Ian's condition continued to worsen. That evening, his mother again called Clifton House and asked that he be admitted. Clifton House regulations, however, preclude admitting anyone under sixteen. Gravely concerned about her son, she then decided to take him to North Memorial Hospital, a highly regarded medical facility located in a suburb of Minneapolis. She changed her mind, however, when the nurse on duty at Clifton House proposed hiring a private Christian Science nurse to provide care for Ian at the McKown home. The services of Quinna Lamb, a private Christian Science nurse, were secured.[2] She arrived at the McKown home later that evening and commenced caring for him. Ian, who had juvenile-onset diabetes—a condition that can usually be treated successfully by administering insulin—died a few hours later.[3]

Kathleen and William McKown were charged with second-degree criminal manslaughter. A district court, however, dismissed the indictments, a decision affirmed by the Court of Appeals of Minnesota and the Minnesota Supreme Court. The court of appeals noted that while the Minnesota child neglect law states that "a parent, legal guardian, or caretaker who willfully deprives a child of . . . health care . . . is guilty of neglect of a child," the statute also specifies that if the person responsible for the child's care "in good faith selects and depends upon spiritual means or prayer for treatment or care of disease or remedial care of the child, this treatment shall constitute 'health care.'"[4]

The courts, however, were not finished with the matter. Ian's father, Douglass G. Lundman, filed a wrongful death civil suit against Ian's mother and stepfather, the Christian Science nurse who had cared for Ian, the Christian Science practitioner Ian's mother hired, the church official who had been consulted, Clifton House, and the First Church of Christ Scientist.[5]

CASE B: PARENTAL REFUSAL TO GIVE
PERMISSION FOR BLOOD TRANSFUSIONS

Fifteen-year-old Kevin Sampson had von Recklinghousen's disease (neurofibromatosis), which resulted in massive disfigurement of the right side of his face and neck. The condition was not life threatening, nor had it progressed to the point that it affected his sight or hearing. However, the grotesque facial disfigurement made him very self-conscious and so adversely affected him psychologically that he had been exempt from school for several years, the result being that he was virtually illiterate. The unanimous recommendation from the wide range of professionals who had dealt with Kevin's case—among them educators, psychologists, psychiatrists, physicians, and surgeons—was that surgery be performed to remove the tumor and restore his facial features to the extent possible. Kevin's mother, Mildred Sampson, gave her permission for the surgery, including the use of plasma,[6] but as a devout Jehovah's Witness, would not authorize blood transfusions.[7] Given the size of the tumor, the surgeons they consulted concluded that to attempt to perform the surgery without the use of blood transfusions posed an unacceptable level of risk. A judge in a family court ordered that "this technically 'neglected' boy be released to the custody of his mother under the supervision of the county Commissioner of Social Services . . . on condition that she cooperate fully with the Department of Social Services in the department's effort to alleviate the boy's neurofibromatosis, and that she permit such surgery and such blood transfusions as duly qualified surgeons may advise or require." The judge further specified that the cost of the surgery and hospitalization should be borne by the county.[8] Kevin's mother refused to go along with the directive of the family court judge and appealed the decision.[9]

CASE C: CERTAIN AND PAINFUL DEATH IF LEFT UNTREATED

An orthopedic surgeon treating twelve-year-old Pamela Hamilton for a fracture of her femur discovered a problem that proved to be Ewing's sarcoma. Medical experts who were consulted were guarded in their prognosis but indicated that if the cancer had not spread, aggressively treating the tumor with radiation and chemotherapy offered a 25 percent to 50 percent chance of long-term remission. If the cancer had spread, the odds of radiation and chemotherapy effecting long-term remission dropped to less than 25 percent, though radiation therapy could provide pain relief. Medical experts were unanimous in stating that if the tumor was left untreated, Pamela would experience a painful death within six to nine months.

Though the medical experts all advocated treating the tumor with radiation and chemotherapy, Pamela's father, Larry T. Hamilton, a lay minister of the Church of God of the Union Assembly, refused permission for the treatment. While allowing medical treatment such as setting fractured bones, suturing wounds, and extracting teeth, the church forbids its members to use medicine, vaccinations, or shots of any kind. Rather than depend on medicine of any type, members of the church are taught to live by faith.

A trial judge, acting on a request submitted to the court by Tennessee's Department of Human Services, determined that as a result of her father's refusal to authorize the treatment, Pamela was "a dependent and neglected child" under Tennessee law and ordered that she be treated. Her father appealed the decision.[10]

CASE D: REFUSING PERMISSION
TO CONTINUE LIFE-SAVING THERAPY

Gerald and Diana Green were living in Hastings, Nebraska, when their son, Chad, then twenty months old, awoke with a temperature of 106 degrees. They immediately took Chad to their family physician, who, after examining him, suspected he might have leukemia and referred him to the Omaha University Medical Center, where the illness was diagnosed as acute lymphocytic leukemia. Chad was admitted to a hospital in Omaha where an intensive program of chemotherapy was begun. Bone marrow tests a month later indicated that the leukemia was in remission.

In part because of their concern about the type of treatment that Chad was being given, which included the possibility of cranial radiation, the Greens decided to move to Scituate, Massachusetts, which was Gerald Green's hometown. Shortly after the move to Massachusetts, they met with Dr. John T. Truman, chief of pediatric hematology at Massachusetts General Hospital, who indicated that cranial radiation would not be necessary and discussed with them the chances for a cure with chemotherapy. He indicated that he was willing to accommodate the Greens' request that Chad be placed on a diet of distilled water, vegetarian foods, and vitamins throughout treatment. He added, however, that while such a diet might be useful during chemotherapy, it would have no value if used alone to treat leukemia. The Greens decided to entrust Chad's care to Dr. Truman.[11]

The anticancer drugs did their job. Bone marrow tests indicated that the leukemia was in complete remission, and the treatment program moved to the long-term maintenance phase. As a result of the treatment, Chad experienced some side effects such as stomach cramps, which were alleviated by adjusting the dosage of his medication. He did not, however, experience many of the side effects often associated with antileukemia drugs—side effects such as headaches, temporary loss of hair, back and joint pain, numbness of fingers and toes, stiffness of the neck, and irritation of the tissues surrounding the spinal column.

During a regularly scheduled visit to Massachusetts General Hospital as the treatment was entering the maintenance phase, the Greens asked what would happen if chemotherapy were terminated. Dr. Truman stated that the chance of a relapse would be 100 percent.

The leukemia recurred three months later. Diana Green admitted that they had discontinued giving Chad the medication they were supposed to give him as part of the chemotherapy program. Dr. Truman informed them that while the likelihood of a cure was diminished by the interruption of the treatment, the possibility of putting the leukemia back into long-term remission still existed, provided that the chemotherapy was resumed. The parents refused permission for the resumption of the chemotherapy. Over a period of several days, Dr. Truman attempted to persuade them to allow resumption of the treatment. They refused. Failing to persuade the Greens to allow resumption of the chemotherapy, Dr. Truman and officials at Massachusetts General Hospital petitioned a court to authorize treatment over the objections of the parents.[12]

FREEDOM TO BELIEVE AND FREEDOM TO ACT

The first three cases are particularly difficult because they involve questions of religious belief and practice—questions that raise First Amendment issues related to freedom of religion, one of the most cherished of all of our constitutionally guaranteed liberties. In *Cantwell et al. v. Connecticut*, a case decided by the U.S. Supreme Court in 1940, Justice Owen Roberts, who delivered the opinion of the Court, made a distinction between freedom to believe and freedom to act. Commenting on the First Amendment, he stated, "Thus the Amendment embraces two concepts—freedom to believe and freedom to act. The first is absolute in the nature of things, the second cannot be. Conduct remains subject to regulation for the protection of society."[13]

The distinction is a valid one. At the same time, however, it should be noted that the line of demarcation between religious belief and religious practice, between the faiths we affirm and the way that we live our lives, cannot always be drawn with complete precision. The faiths that we affirm must give form and direction to our lives, or else they are not really faith at all. Faith is not detached belief, assent without action. Faith by its very nature compels action.[14]

But though the line between religious belief and practice, between the faiths that we affirm and the way that we live our lives, cannot always be drawn precisely, that does not by implication suggest that respect for freedom of religion mandates tolerance for anything done in the name of religion. In the *Cantwell* decision, Justice Roberts put it this way: "Under the constitutional guaranty, freedom of conscience and of religious belief is absolute, although freedom to act in the exercise of religion is subject to regulation for the protection of society. Such regulation, however, in attaining a permissible end, must not unduly infringe the protected freedom."

JUDICIAL INTERVENTION

When the question of judicial intervention comes up in religiously based cases involving parental refusal of beneficial medical treatment for their children, frequent reference is made to *Prince v. Massachusetts*,[15] a case decided by the U.S. Supreme Court in 1944.[16] Justice Wiley B. Rutledge, who delivered the opinion of the Court, observed, "It is cardinal with us that the custody, care and nurture of the child reside first in the parents, whose primary function and freedom include preparation for obligations the state can neither supply nor hinder. . . . But the family itself is not beyond regulation in the public interest, as against a claim of religious liberty." Justice Rutledge further noted that "the state has a wide range of power for limiting parental freedom and authority in things affecting the child's welfare; and that this includes, to some extent, matters of conscience and religious conviction." As for types of activity that might be harmful to individuals, he concluded, in a passage that has been widely quoted, "Parents may be free to become martyrs themselves. But it does not follow they are free, in identical circumstances, to make martyrs of their children before they have reached the age of full and legal discretion when they can make that choice for themselves."[17]

Two observations about the *Prince* decision, however, are in order. First of all, it had nothing at all to do with medical treatment.[18] Sarah Prince was arrested for violating a Massachusetts law prohibiting any boy under the age of twelve or any girl under the age of eighteen from selling in public places newspapers, periodicals, or any other articles of merchandise. The law further made it unlawful for anyone to provide minors with articles to sell and for any parent or guardian to permit a minor to work in violation of the law. Prince had custody of her nine-year-old niece, Betty M. Simmons, who joined her in distributing Jehovah's Witness publications in Brockton, Massachusetts. The U.S. Supreme Court upheld the lower court decision convicting Prince of violating the Massachusetts law.[19]

Second, *Prince* was far from a unanimous decision. Making reference to the distribution of religious literature in the public streets, Justice Frank Murphy stated in his dissenting view, "If the right of a child to practice its religion in that manner is to be forbidden by constitutional means, there must be convincing proof that such a practice constitutes a grave and immediate danger to the state or to the health, morals or welfare of the child."[20] Indeed, Justice Rutledge himself, who provided the swing vote in the five–four decision and wrote the opinion of the Court, reportedly stated some time after the decision that he had been tempted to flip a coin to determine his vote and that he almost wrote the decision "the other way"—that is, to overturn the Superior Court of Massachusetts decision convicting Sarah Prince of violating the state statute, rather than affirming the lower court decision.[21]

But notwithstanding the rather murky nature of the *Prince* decision, it has become a frequent reference point in discussions of whether intervention is in order in cases in which parents object to potentially beneficial medical treatment for their children. And indeed, in some situations there is a case to be made for intervention. It bears noting that even Justice Murphy in his dissent allows that intervention is in order if there is "grave and immediate danger . . . to the health, morals or welfare of the child."

COMPETING PRIMA FACIE OBLIGATIONS

But though intervention might sometimes be justifiable, it is something that ought to be done with great reluctance and only as a last resort. Furthermore, it must be done only if the benefits to be gained are sufficient to offset the costs such as those to the autonomy of the parents, to the integrity of the family, and to the practice of religious freedom. To put this in slightly different words, it is plausible to argue that health care professionals and others involved in these situations have an obligation to be concerned not only about the well-being of the child but also about the rights and autonomy of the parents. In short, there is both a prima facie obligation to do what is in the best interests of the child and a prima facie obligation to respect the preferences and beliefs of the child's parents.

When confronted with competing prima facie obligations, the first thing we typically do, be it in cases of this sort or in any other situation, is to attempt to eliminate the conflict. Sometimes this can be done. Sometimes there are treatment options that offer prospects for successfully treating a child's illness or injury without violating the preferences and beliefs of the parents. A policy statement issued by the American Academy of Pediatrics calls on those entrusted with the care of children to "show sensitivity to and flexibility toward the religious beliefs and the practices of families."[22]

Dr. Carolyn Roy-Bornstein and Dr. Linda D. Sagor were treating a fourteen-month-old child with Kawasaki syndrome, a disease that results in inflammation of coronary arteries and other blood vessels. The parents of the child were Jehovah's Witnesses who objected to blood transfusions. In conversations with the parents, Dr. Roy-Bornstein and Dr. Sagor raised the possibility of using immune globulin rather than whole blood. When the parents expressed concern about the compatibility of this treatment with their religious beliefs, the discussion was expanded to include local church elders and senior members of the Watch Tower Bible and Tract Society in Brooklyn, New York. The conclusion reached after many hours of discussion was that the treatment was acceptable, and the child was successfully treated.[23] The way that the doctors approached this case was both appropriate and responsible.

With the development of blood substitutes, intraoperative blood salvage techniques, plasma expanders, and many other new products and procedures, there often are alternatives to blood transfusions.[24] David Malyon, a Jehovah's Witness who chairs a hospital liaison committee at a hospital in England, asserts, "The charges against our views in a medical context are clearly out of date! Our faithful adherence to Biblical tenets has resulted in the development of new surgical and medical techniques to obviate the use of blood therapy, which are in the very forefront of medical developments."[25]

At the same time, it bears noting that what might appear to be an elegant solution to a difficult problem sometimes falls short of resolving the conflict between the prima facie obligation to be concerned about the well-being of the child and the prima facie obligation to be respectful of the preferences and beliefs of the child's parents. Sometimes alternate forms of therapy are not available, or, if available, sometimes they do not offer significant prospects for success. When the conflict between competing prima facie obligations cannot be eliminated, priorities must be established. In such situations, the case for intervention must be weighed in relation to other considerations, such as respect for the integrity of the family, parental autonomy, and religious freedom.

INTERVENTION AND THE
TRADITIONAL JUST WAR CRITERIA

Though originally formulated to provide ethical guidance in an entirely different type of situation, the traditional just war criteria—just cause, right intent, last resort, lawful authority, reasonable hope of success, and proportionality—provide useful guidelines for determining when intervention is warranted mandating treatment in violation of religiously based parental objections. Because of the restraints built into these guidelines, they are principles of reluctant intervention, yet they also suggest that intervention is sometimes the lesser of evils.

Just as the criterion of just cause insists that morally significant reasons are essential when justifying war, intervention overriding parental objections to beneficial medical treatment should be done only if there is a morally significant reason for doing so. Many would support judicial intervention if the life of the child is at risk. Take, for example, the aforementioned case of Pamela Hamilton. The Court of Appeals of Tennessee, Eastern Section, designated the director of the Offices of Human Services in Knoxville to act on her behalf and authorized him to consent on her behalf to necessary treatment for her cancer. The court stated,

> Our Constitution guarantees Americans more personal freedom than enjoyed by any other civilized society, but there are times when the freedom of the individual must yield. Where a child is dying with cancer and experiencing pain which will surely become more excruciating as the disease progresses, as in Pamela's circumstance, we believe, is one of those times when humane considerations and life-saving attempts outweigh unlimited practices of religious beliefs.[26]

And so if the life of the child is at risk, the case for intervention is a fairly strong one. But what if the condition is not life threatening? That was the issue in the case of Kevin Sampson. The Court of Appeals of New York affirmed the lower court order mandating that blood transfusions be permitted and providing that the cost of surgery and hospitalization should be covered by the county. The court of appeals stated that courts have power "to direct surgery even in the absence of risk to the physical health or life of the subject or to the public." The court further stated, "Nor does the religious objection to blood transfusion present a bar at least where the transfusion is necessary to the success of required surgery."[27] The argument made by the court of appeals has much to recommend it.

Right Intent

The criterion of right intent has received relatively little attention in discussions regarding cases of judicial intervention. But like the other just war criteria, it is of significance. Whether the criterion is applied to the question of going to war or to the question of intervention to mandate beneficial medical treatment for children, intervening ought to be done for the right reasons. Sometimes there are hidden agendas. The reasons publicly given for going to war do not always form the real reason that military action is taken. Similarly, intervention overriding religiously based parental objections can derive from dislike of the parents' religious views rather from the professed concern for the well-being of the child. Intervention is justifiable, however, only for the right reasons: concern for the well-being of the child is a morally defensible reason; distaste for the religious views of the parents is not.

Last Resort

As in the case of decisions to go to war, intervention overriding religiously based parental objections is justifiable only if it is the last resort. Just as it is possible to be too quick to go to war, so also it is possible to be too quick to intervene. *Prince v. Massachusetts* should be kept on the back burner rather than serve as the departure point for the decision-making process.

Appropriate use of the criterion of last resort is illustrated by a case involving an infant with hypoplastic left heart syndrome who was treated at the Maine Medical Center in Portland, Maine. When the child's parents, who are Jehovah's Witnesses, objected to blood transfusions, the surgeon promised the parents that the surgical team would make every effort to perform the surgery without blood or blood products. However, the parents were also informed that the hospital would petition a court for authorization to use blood transfusions if the situation became critical. The court order clearly specified the circumstances under which transfusions could be administered. The surgery was successfully performed without the use of blood or blood products. But when the patient's condition deteriorated significantly as he was weaned from the cardiopulmonary bypass circuit, it became clear to the surgical team that the effort to treat his condition without blood could not be sustained, and he was transfused. Subsequent stages of the surgical process were successfully accomplished without transfusions.[28]

The surgical team did the right thing when, in keeping with the preferences of the parents, they attempted to perform the surgery without transfusions. They also did the right thing by stating up front that they would give transfusions if necessary to save the life of the child and by getting a court order authorizing them to do so. And they did the right thing when they transfused the infant when the situation became critical and his life was at risk. Transfusing the infant, albeit in violation of the preferences of the parents, was in this situation the lesser of evils.

Lawful Authority

When a decision is made to intervene, it should be via established legal channels with rigorous adherence to due process. Once again, the Maine Medical Center case provides a morally praiseworthy example of the appropriate way to proceed. Perhaps a case can be made for stopping short of insisting that securing a court order is an absolute precondition for intervention; for example, in an emergency situation in which a child is bleeding profusely, doctors may not have time to secure a court order before having to administer a blood transfusion. However, wisdom is surely on the side of seeking court approval—if possible and as expeditiously as possible—and refraining from intervention if appropriate legal authorities refuse to approve the proposed intervention.

Reasonable Hope of Success

Because intervention is always costly, it is justifiable only if there is reason to believe that the problem can be resolved by intervention. A case where timely intervention might have saved the life of a child is that of Ian Lundman noted earlier. He had juvenile-onset diabetes, a condition that can usually be treated successfully by administering insulin.

Ensuring access to insulin in the case of a child with juvenile-onset diabetes is a relatively simple example where the prospects of success, measured in terms of saving the life of the child, are virtually 100 percent. Other cases, such as the use of experimental forms of chemotherapy to treat childhood forms of cancer, are more problematic since the outcome is far more uncertain. The bar that must be hurdled to make the case for intervention is much higher in these cases. Yet, as illustrated by the example of Pamela Hamilton, a compelling case for intervention can be made in some situations in which the probabilities of success are 50 percent or less, particularly if the life of the child is at risk and death is certain if the child is left untreated.

Proportionality

This last point brings us to the last of the traditional just war criteria as they apply to cases involving parental refusal of beneficial medical treatment for their children—the notion of proportionality. Just as war is always a costly option, so also is intervention to override parental refusal. Intervention does violence to the integrity of the family and, in some cases, to the practice of religion as well, matters that ought not be taken lightly in a society that affirms both the integrity of the family and freedom of religion. What this means in practical terms is that a sufficient amount of good must reasonably be expected to result from intervention to offset the costs, emotional and otherwise, that are imposed on the parents who refuse permission.[29] If the life of the child is at risk and treatment is available that offers significant prospects for success, the case for intervention is relatively easy to make, for saving the life of a child can offset a mountain of harm to the autonomy and religious freedom of the parents. However, if the benefits to the child are either lesser in magnitude or less certain, the case for intervention is far more difficult to make, if indeed it can be made at all. For example, intervention is surely not warranted in cases in which parents, for religious reasons, refuse to allow their daughters to wear makeup, even if some might argue that such refusal is harmful to the girls' self-image. Other cases, both hypothetical and actual, fall somewhere between these two ends of the spectrum.

And what if alternate therapy does not offer the same prospects for success as conventional therapy? While no precise mathematical formula is available to calculate risk factors and various probabilities for success, modest reductions in the probability of success can be morally acceptable as an alternative to mandating treatment over the objections of parents. Factors to be considered in such cases include the following:

1. Is the situation life threatening for the child?

2. How significant is the differential in the probabilities of success for the alternate therapy compared with conventional therapy?

3. How strong are the parental objections? Are the parents adamantly opposed to conventional therapy? Or do they simply prefer that it not be used?

ALLOCATING COSTS

There is one final matter that remains to be addressed—allocating costs related to alternate forms of therapy. The costs can be substantial, both in financial terms and in terms of time demands on physicians and other health care professionals. For example, in the aforementioned case of the child with Kawasaki syndrome, the doctors spent a substantial amount of time in conversation with the child's parents and in discussions with local church elders and senior members of the Watch Tower Bible and Tract Society, time that could have been spent with other patients—or with their own families.

Simon Finfer, who now practices in Australia but previously was a trauma surgeon at a hospital in the United Kingdom, has charged that because alternatives to blood transfusions are expensive, their use diverts resources that might be used for the care of other patients.[30] In an article that appeared in the *Hastings Center Report*, Stephen G. Post expresses concern about costs imposed on others, commenting on a case involving a Jehovah's Witness with an ectopic pregnancy who refused blood transfusions but whose life was saved by an expensive alternate procedure. (The cost of the procedure was absorbed by the hospital.) He writes, "Nevertheless, in a just health care system, believers who reject the wider society's accepted standards of medical futility, definitions of death, and blood use have no claim on nonbelievers for a financial blank check. The individual or sect holding an expensive belief must pay for it. Otherwise, the wider society is held hostage to any and all creeds."[31] Commenting on the same case, Leonard Fleck adds, "If $100,000 is spent to meet the needs of one patient, as in this case, then those resources are not available for meeting the health needs of other uninsured individuals who may also need health care from that institution."[32]

In short, the prima facie obligation to seek out alternate forms of treatment that eliminate the conflict between the obligation to save a patient's life and the obligation to respect religious views can conflict with another prima facie obligation—that of helping others who need health care. Granted, this conflict can be eliminated if Jehovah's Witnesses and others who object to conventional forms of therapy purchase additional insurance to cover the costs of expensive alternate forms of therapy. But what if they are unwilling or unable to pay for this coverage? Fleck observes, "We might be tempted to argue that if individually or collectively they failed to choose or create an effective insurance scheme for this purpose then this is no fault of society at large, and hence, health providers can in good conscience deny them the care that they seek and allow them to die. This is what a free society is all about." However, he adds that there is a consistency problem with this approach. He notes that "there are very many young adults who foolishly fail to purchase health insurance, who are in serious automobile accidents, and whose lives can be saved and restored through timely expensive medical interventions. We do not punish them for their foolishness by simply allowing them to die in our emergency rooms once it has been determined that they are without health insurance and without ability to pay for the care they need."

It might be added that a socialized system of health care such as the United Kingdom's National Health System does not eliminate the problem. In such a system—some would say particularly in such a system— allocation decisions still have to be made. As Finfer correctly points out, providing expensive alternate therapy for one patient can leave the health system without the funds needed to treat other patients.

There is no comfortable solution to this dilemma. It is tempting to say that because freedom of conscience is such an important value in our society, we should all be willing to chip in a bit to help pay for alternate therapy for those who lack the insurance coverage or funds to pay for this therapy. But however plausible that might be on a theoretical level, it is a position that is difficult to sustain on the practical level. In an era in which the health insurance business has become intensively competitive as employers desperately seek to restrain ballooning health benefit costs for their employees, building in a little extra to help pay for alternate therapy for those who failed to buy additional insurance is not likely to happen.

Where does this leave us? Encouraging Jehovah's Witnesses and others who refuse standard therapy to buy additional insurance to cover the added costs of alternate forms of therapy is certainly in order. But if they fail to do this and lack the funds to pay for expensive alternate therapy, there is no solution that does not cause as many problems as it resolves. Depriving other patients of needed care to cover the cost of expensive forms of alternate care is not a morally comfortable option. Neither is allowing children to die when their lives can be saved.

Perhaps the following guideline can be useful when attempting to resolve these troubling situations: to the extent that funds can be made available for alternate therapy without adversely affecting the care received by other patients, priority ought to be given to treating minors whose parents object to conventional care. It is one thing to ask adults to bear the consequences of the decisions they make. It is quite another to let children bear the consequences of the decisions their parents make in situations in which amelioration is possible.

THE REST OF THE STORY

What happened in the four cases noted at the beginning of this chapter? In the case involving Ian Lundman, the Court of Appeals of Minnesota ruled that Ian's mother, his stepfather, Quinna Lamb (the Christian Science nurse hired to care for him), and Mario Tosto (the Christian Science practitioner hired to pray for him) all had a duty to care for him. However, the duty to care for Ian did not extend to James Van Horn (the church official consulted), Clifton House (the Christian Science Nursing home consulted), or the First Church of Christ, Scientist. The court concluded,

The undisputed facts show that Ian's caregivers failed to seek medical help in the three days leading to his death, despite continuous and dramatic indications that Ian was ill with a life-threatening disease—first seriously, then gravely—and that he would die, given continued reliance on Christian Science prayer. The undisputed facts indicated that appellants had no lawful choice but to seek medical help. We hold as a matter of law, therefore, that the four duty-bound defendants breached the standard of care for a reasonable Christian Scientist, who was obligated—with knowledge of a child's grave illness—to seek the assistance of conventional medicine. Further, their separate breaches of duty proximately caused Ian's death.[33]

In the case of Kevin Sampson, the Court of Appeals of New York affirmed the lower court order mandating that blood transfusions be permitted, if needed for the corrective surgery, and providing that the cost of surgery and hospitalization should be covered by the county. The court of appeals stated that courts have power "to direct surgery even in the absence of risk to the physical health or life of the subject or to the public." The court further stated, "Nor does the religious objection to blood transfusion present a bar at least where the transfusion is necessary to the success of required surgery."[34]

As mentioned, in the case of Pamela Hamilton, the court of appeals authorized the Offices of Human Services to act on Pamela's behalf and give consent for her treatment.

In the case of Chad Green, the Probate Court for Plymouth County, Massachusetts, granted Dr. Truman's request that a temporary guardian be appointed who could authorize treatment. That was done, and Chad was brought to Massachusetts General Hospital for treatment. After questions were raised about the authority of the probate court to authorize treatment, Dr. Truman filed a petition in the Second District Court of Plymouth requesting that the Department of Public Welfare be given legal custody of Chad for the limited purpose of providing necessary care. The district court judge dismissed the petition. Dr. Truman and Chad's court-appointed counsel then appealed to the Superior Court, where a judge found Chad in need of care and protection and gave legal custody to the Department of Public Welfare for the express purpose of receiving chemotherapy. The judge ruled that his parents had physical custody of him, meaning that he would remain with them as long as they obeyed the order of the court. The Supreme Judicial Court of Massachusetts, on its own initiative, ordered appellate review. After reviewing the case, the court affirmed the Superior Court decision.[35]

That, however, was not the end of the matter. Defying the court order, Chad's parents took him to Mexico, where he was treated with laetrile and placed on a special diet. The chemotherapy was discontinued. Chad died nine months after arriving in Mexico. A Massachusetts court found Chad's parents guilty of criminal contempt but imposed no punishment, concluding that they had suffered enough.[36] The Greens returned to Nebraska, where they had two more children. Ten years after Chad's death, they divorced. Both subsequently remarried.[37]

Four sad and tragic cases indeed.

SOME CONCLUDING CONSIDERATIONS

Taken together, the cases of Ian Lundman, Kevin Sampson, Pamela Hamilton, and Chad Green underscore the depth of anguish that these situations invariably involve—anguish stemming from the fact that parents in all four cases sincerely believed they were doing what was best for their children. Anguish intensified by the fact that standard forms of medical treatment were available—treatment that could have significantly improved their children's chances of survival.

To summarize, intervention overriding parental objections should be done only as a last resort and with great reluctance since intervention of this sort is an intrusion on the integrity of the family and does not sit comfortably with the notion of religious freedom. For this reason, efforts should always be made to find alternatives to intervention, be they alternate forms of therapy or gentle persuasion directed toward attaining parental approval for conventional forms of therapy. But in some cases, alternatives are not identifiable. And in some of these cases, when the criteria of just cause, right intent, last resort, lawful authority, reasonable hope of success, and proportionality are satisfied, intervention can be the lesser of evils. Just as war is sometimes the lesser of evils but should always be done with regret and remorse, so also should intervention overriding parental refusal of medical treatment for their children always be done with regret and remorse—but resolutely when the scales of morality tip in favor of intervention.

NOTES

1. *Lundman v. McKown et al.,* Court of Appeals of Minnesota, 530 N.W.2d 807 (1995).

2. Additional information about Christian Science nurses can be found at the website sponsored by the Association of Oranizations for Christian Science Nursing, www.aocsn.org/TheCSNurse.htm (accessed November 9, 2002).

3. *Lundman v. McKown et al.* (1995).

4. *State v. McKown,* Court of Appeals of Minnesota, 461 N.W.2d 720 (1990). Other state courts have reached different decisions in cases involving Christian Scientists. A few years before the McKown case, Laurie Grouard Walker was indicted for involuntary manslaughter and convicted by a California court as a result of the dealth of her four-year-old daughter from meningitis. Walker had secured the services of a Christian Science practitioner and a Christian Science nurse to care for her daughter but had not sought conventional medical care. Walker's conviction was upheld by the Supreme Court of California (*Laurie Grouard Walker v. the Superior Court of Sacramento County,* Supreme Court of California, 47 Cal. 3d 112 [1988]). In *Commonwealth v. David R. Twitchell* and *Commonwealth v. Ginger Twitchell* (416 Mass. 114 [1993]), the Supreme Judicial Court of Massachusetts upheld the convictions

of David and Ginger Twitchell for involuntary manslaughter pertaining to the death of their two-and-a-half-year-old son from peritonitis resulting from perforation of the bowel. The court ruled that the spiritual exemption clause in Massachusetts's medical neglect statute did not protect the Twitchells from criminal liability. A Florida case, however, had a different outcome. Like the Walker and Twitchell cases, the Hermanson case involved Christian Scientist parents who were indicted on criminal charges and convicted. However, in *William Hermanson and Christine Hermanson v. State of Florida*, 604 So.2d 775 (1992), the Supreme Court of Florida overturned the convictions, primarily on grounds of due process. The court stated that "the legislature has failed to clearly indicate the point at which a parent's reliance on his or her religious beliefs in the treatment of his or her children becomes criminal conduct."

5. *Lundman v. McKown et al.* (1995).

6. *In re Kevin Sampson*, Family Court of New York, Ulster County, 65 Misc. 2d 658 (1970).

7. Jehovah's Witnesses' objection to blood transfusions derives from their interpretation (which is not shared by other religious groups) of certain biblical passages that prohibit eating blood, among them Genesis 9:3–4, Deuteronomy 12:23–25, and Leviticus 17:13–14. The group's views on blood transfusions are outlined in a brochure entitled *How Can Blood Save Your Life?* at www.watchtower.org/library/hb/index.htm (accessed January 26, 2003).

8. *In re Kevin Sampson* (1970).

9. *In re Kevin Sampson*, Court of Appeals of New York, 29 Y.Y.2d 900 (1972).

10. *In re Hamilton*, Court of Appeals of Tennessee, Eastern Section, 657 S.W.2d 425 (1983).

11. *Custody of a Minor*, Supreme Judicial Court of Massachusetts, 375 Mass. 733 (1978); Philip M. Boffey, "Spare the Parents, Kill the Child?" *New York Times*, December 15, 1980, A22.

12. *Custody of a Minor* (1978).

13. *Cantwell et al. v. Connecticut*, 310 U.S. 296 (1940). The case involved three Jehovah's Witnesses—Newton Cantwell and his two sons, Jesse and Russell—who had been arrested for attempting to persuade residents of a predominantly Roman Catholic neighborhood in New Haven, Connecticut, to accept their religious beliefs. They were charged with violating a Connecticut law that prohibited soliciting nonmembers for any religious cause without the approval of the secretary of the public welfare council. The Court overturned

their convictions. Speaking for the Court, Justice Roberts wrote, "The State is . . . free to regulate the time and manner of solicitation generally, in the interest of public safety, peace, comfort or convenience. But to condition the solicitation of aid for the perpetuation of religious views or systems upon a license, the grant of which rests in the exercise of a determination by state authority as to what is a religious cause, is to lay a forbidden burden upon the exercise of liberty protected by the Constitution." For a narrative of the events that led to the Cantwells' arrests, see Shawn Francis Peters, *Judging Jehovah's Witnesses: Religious Persecution and the Dawn of the Rights Revolution* (Lawrence: University Press of Kansas, 2000), 178–81.

14. This understanding of faith is discussed in greater detail in Daniel E. Lee, *Navigating Right and Wrong: Ethical Decision Making in a Pluralistic Age* (Lanham, Md.: Rowman and Littlefield, 2002), esp. 89, 120–21, 130–32.

15. *Prince v. Massachusetts*, 321 U.S. 158 (1944). Because the war news dominated front pages in 1944, relatively little attention was paid to the decision at the time. The report of the decision was buried on page 22 of the February 1, 1944, edition of the *New York Times* (Lewis Wood, "Jehovahites Lose in Supreme Court: Decision, 5 to 4, Sustains State in Barring Minors from Sale of Pamphlets in Street," *New York Times*, February 1, 1944, 22).

16. See, for example, *Jehovah's Witnesses in the State of Washington et al. v. King County Hospital Unit No. 1 (Harborview) et al.*, United States District Court for the Western District of Washington, Northern Division, 278 F. Supp. 488 (1967); *In re Kevin Sampson*, Family Court of New York, Ulster County, 65 Misc. 2d 658 (1970); *In re D.L.E.*, Supreme Court of Colorado, 645 P.2d 271 (1982); *Staelens v. Yake*, United States District Court for the Northern District of Illinois, Western Division, 432 F. Supp. 834 (1977); *Lundman v. McKown*, Court of Appeals of Minnesota, 530 N.W.2d 807 (1995); and *Walker v. Superior Court of Sacramento County*, Supreme Court of California, 762 P.2d 852 (1988). *In re Kevin Sampson* and *Staelens v. Yake* pertained to Jehovah's Witnesses. *In re D.L.E., Lundman v. McKown,* and *Walker v. Superior Court of Sacramento County* addressed issues related to medical treatment for children of Christian Scientists.

17. *Prince v. Massachusetts* (1944).

18. Neither did *Cantwell et al. v. Connecticut.* See note 13.

19. For a narrative of events related to the decision, see Peters, *Judging Jehovah's Witnesses*, 198–202.

20. *Prince v. Massachusetts* (1944).

21. Peters, *Judging Jehovah's Witnesses*, 199.

22. American Academy of Pediatrics Committee on Bioethics, "Religious Objections to Medical Care (RE9707)," *Pediatrics* 99, no. 2 (February 1997): 279–81, at www.aap.org/policy/re9707.html (accessed December 8, 2003).

23. Carolyn Roy-Bornstein and Linda D. Sagor, "Treatment of a Jehovah's Witness with Immune Globulin: Case of a Child with Kawasaki Syndrome," *Pediatrics* 94, no. 1 (July 1994): 112.

24. A number of alternatives are noted in *How Can Blood Save Your Life?* See also "Jehovah's Witnesses: The Surgical/Ethical Challenge," *Journal of the American Medical Association* 246, no. 21 (November 27, 1981): 2471–72; and J. Lowell Dixon, "Blood: Whose Choice and Whose Conscience," *New York State Journal of Medicine* 88 (1988): 463–64.

25. David Malyon, "Transfusion-Free Treatment of Jehovah's Witnesses: Respecting the Autonomous Patient's Motives," *Journal of Medical Ethics* 24, no. 6 (December 1998): 376–81.

26. *In re Hamilton* (1983).

27. *In re Kevin Sampson* (1972).

28. Richard J. Forest, Robert C. Groom, Reed Quinn, Jon Donnelly, and Cantwell Clark, "Repair of Hypoplastic Left Heart Syndrome of a 4.25-kg Jehovah's Witness," *Perfusion* 17 (2002): 221–25.

29. When I presented a paper based on this chapter at the Forty-fifth Annual Meeting of the Society of Christian Ethics held in Chicago, January 8–11, 2004, Thomas A. Shannon, who was in attendance, noted in very moving terms the deep sense of harm experienced by parents who are Jehovah's Witnesses when their children are given blood transfusions over their objections.

30. Noted by Ross Kessel, *Hastings Center Report* 25, no. 1 (January/February 1995): 3.

31. Stephen G. Post and Leonard Fleck, "My Conscience, Your Money," *Hastings Center Report* 25, no. 5 (September/October 1995): 28–29.

32. Post and Fleck, "My Conscience, Your Money," 28–29.

33. *Lundman v. McKown et al.* (1995).

34. *In re Kevin Sampson* (1972).

35. *Custody of a Minor* (1978).

36. Boffey, "Spare the Parents, Kill the Child?"

37. "Mother Remembers Legal Battle over Son's Treatment," Associated Press, October 31, 1999.

Ten Questions for Reflection and Discussion

1   Should doctors attempt to persuade parents to allow forms of treatment to which they object?

2   When is it appropriate for doctors to seek court orders over-riding parental objections?

3   To what extent is the case for intervention stronger in life-threatening illness or injury?

4   To what extent is the case for intervention stronger in situations in which parental refusal is not based on religious beliefs?

5   Does the strength (i.e., the depth of feeling) of parental objections make a difference?

6   To what extent is accepting alternate treatments with lesser prospects acceptable in order to avoid violating parental preferences?

7   Who should cover the cost of court-authorized medical treatment?

8   If alternate forms of treatment acceptable to parents are more expensive than conventional care, who should cover the added cost?

9   If parents objecting to conventional care lack the financial resources to cover more expensive alternate care, should hospital funds budgeted for uncompensated care be used to cover the cost of this care?

10 If court-authorized treatment is administered over the objections of parents, what measures might be taken to heal the damage this causes to the cohesiveness of the family?

6

PRIVATE PROPERTY RIGHTS

AND THE ENDANGERED SPECIES ACT

—

In an article that appeared in an environmental periodical, environmental attorney Michael J. Bean reports that staff members of the Land's End Visitor Center on Colorado's Grand Mesa were startled by three visitors, "odd-looking, taciturn types" who "did not ask questions . . . [but] merely looked around and then left without saying a word." Bean adds, "Of course no one really expected them to say anything; they were California condors."[1] A strong supporter of the Endangered Species Act, Bean emphatically believes that the act has helped save the California condor and other endangered species.

Quite a different picture of the Endangered Species Act is painted in an editorial that first appeared in the *Wall Street Journal* and is noted on the website of the National Endangered Species Act Reform Coalition. The editorial reports that Brandt Child bought a five-hundred-acre parcel of land in Utah, only to be told by the U.S. Fish and Wildlife Service that he could not build a campground and golf course on the property because the three lakes were home to an estimated two hundred thousand thumbnail-sized Kanab ambersnails, a federally protected species. When he discovered ten domestic geese near his ponds and dutifully notified federal officials, he was told that he would be subjected to a fine of $50,000 per snail if the geese had eaten any of them. The coalition includes several other stories of a similar genre on its website, all of them intended to call attention to what they perceive as unwarranted infringement on private property rights.[2]

Considered together, these two anecdotes underscore the deep divide between many environmentalists and defenders of private property rights. This clash confronts us with an exceedingly difficult question: To what extent, if at all, is intervention warranted that protects and preserves threatened and endangered species by limiting what property owners can do with their property?

THE ENDANGERED SPECIES ACT OF 1973

Though many today view environmental protection as the domain of the Democratic Party, the Endangered Species Act of 1973 became law during a Republican administration—that of Richard M. Nixon.[3] And it was enacted with broad bipartisan support, with the U.S. Senate voting 99–1 in favor of the bill and with only twelve members of the U.S. House of Representatives voting against it.[4] Upon signing the law, President Nixon stated,

> Nothing is more priceless and more worthy of preservation than the rich array of animal life with which our country has been blessed. It is a many-faceted treasure, of value to scholars, scientists and nature lovers alike and it forms a vital part of the heritage we share as Americans.[5]

While the act has been amended several times—most notably in 1978, 1982, and 1988—the basic provisions of the act have remained essentially unchanged.[6] Using the language of "legalese" that is so typical of legislative measures, the Endangered Species Act of 1973 defines

- "endangered species" as "any species which is in danger of extinction throughout all or a significant portion of its range other than a species of Class Insecta determined by the Secretary [of the Interior] to constitute a pest whose protection under the provisions of this Act would present an overwhelming and overriding risk to man";

- "threatened species" as "any species which is likely to become an endangered species throughout all or a significant portion of its range"; and

- "critical habitat" as "the specific areas within the geographical area occupied by the species . . . on which are found those physical or biological features (I) essential to the conservation of the species and (II) which may require special management."

The act, however, specifies that except in cases involving special circumstances critical habitat "shall not include the entire geographical area which can be occupied by the threatened or endangered species."[7]

The act mandates that that the secretary of the interior "shall by regulation . . . determine whether any species is an endangered species or a threatened species" and that "concurrently with making a determination" shall "designate any habitat of such species which is then considered to be critical habitat . . . on the basis of the best scientific data available and after taking into consideration the economic impact, and any other relevant impact, of specifying any particular area as critical habitat."[8]

The regulatory authority assigned to the secretary of the interior is delegated to the Fish and Wildlife Service while that assigned to the secretary of commerce is delegated to the National Marine Fisheries Service.

THE ACT CHALLENGED

At first, there was little criticism of the Endangered Species Act. After all, who could be opposed to preserving the bald eagle and other icons of our national heritage? But then matters started getting complicated.

The controversy about the Tellico Dam, a project of the Tennessee Valley Authority (TVA) on the Little Tennessee River, marked a turning point in public perception. In 1973, David Etnier of the University of Tennessee discovered a little fish called the snail darter in a portion of the Little Tennessee River that would be affected by the dam. Lynn A. Greenwalt, the head of the Fish and Wildlife Service at the time, advised TVA to halt construction and encouraged them to look in nearby streams for other populations of the snail darter. TVA did neither. In October 1975, the Fish and Wildlife Service listed the little fish as an endangered species on an emergency basis and ruled that TVA could not complete construction of the dam. TVA refused to comply and the case ended up in court. The district court dismissed the case. An appeal was filed. The appellate court ruled that the Endangered Species Act did apply to Tellico and issued an injunction ordering TVA to halt construction on the project, which was 90 percent complete. TVA appealed the case to the U.S. Supreme Court.[9]

The U.S. Supreme Court upheld the appellate court decision. Delivering the opinion of the Court, Chief Justice Warren Burger wrote, "It is clear from the Act's legislative history that Congress intended to halt and reverse the trend toward species extinction, whatever the cost." He further noted, "It may seem curious to some that the survival of a relatively small number of three-inch fish among all the countless millions of species extant would require the permanent halting of a virtually completed dam for which Congress has expended more than $100 million. . . . We conclude, however, that the explicit provisions of the Endangered Species Act require precisely that result."[10]

And so a major construction project was halted by the snail darter, a little fish that few knew about and even fewer cared about, a little fish of no commercial or recreational significance whatsoever, a little fish almost totally lacking in charisma.

The Tellico Dam controversy, which was a clash between two agencies of the federal government, did not involve private property rights (though it did have some implications for property owners hoping to benefit from the project). Yet, in a very direct and dramatic way, it illustrated the impact the Endangered Species Act could have. And it made very clear that the act pertained not just to bald eagles and other high-profile creatures but to obscure plants and animals as well.

THE ENDANGERED SPECIES ACT
AND PRIVATE PROPERTY RIGHTS

Controversy involving private property rights was not far down the road. While the Fish and Wildlife Service initially focused its efforts on preserving critical habitat in national forests and on other publicly held land, in the 1980s regulatory intervention was extended to private property as well.[11] When this happened, the Endangered Species Act, which had been almost universally applauded at its birth, became the center of heated controversy, as good will gave way to anger and hostility.

In the 1990s the Clinton administration placed restrictions on logging old-growth forest (including on some parcels that were privately owned) to protect the habitat of the northern spotted owl, a threatened species, and the red-cockaded woodpecker, an endangered species. A consortium of timber industry representatives and private property owners took legal action. In *Babbitt v. Sweet Home Chapter of Communities for a Great Oregon*, lawyers representing the consortium charged that the secretary of the interior had overstepped his authority by interpreting the Endangered Species Act's prohibition of harm to threatened and endangered species as including "significant habitat modification or degradation" that kills or injures threatened and endangered species by "significantly impairing essential behavioral patterns, including breeding, feeding or sheltering."

The district court ruled against the petitioners, but the United States Court of Appeals for the District of Columbia reversed the lower court decision, with a majority of the court of appeals (upon rehearing the case) concluding that the secretary of the interior had exceeded the authority granted by the Endangered Species Act. The case was appealed to the U.S. Supreme Court.

In a six–three decision, the Supreme Court reversed the court of appeals decision. The Court concluded that the secretary of the interior had not exceeded his authority by interpreting the Endangered Species Act as prohibiting certain types of habitat modification detrimental to endangered and threatened species. Moreover, the Court stated that the Endangered Species Act applies "to all land in the United States," not just land in the public domain. Thus, the Court gave legal sanction to regulatory intervention to prevent destruction of critical habitat on private property.[12]

TAKINGS?

The matter was not yet fully resolved. Private property rights advocates turned to the "takings" provision of the Fifth Amendment to claim a right to compensation for any diminished value to private property resulting from regulatory intervention limiting its use. The Fifth Amendment provides that no person shall be "deprived of life, liberty, or property, without due process of law; nor shall private property be taken for public use, without just compensation." The Fifth Amendment is widely (and appropriately) interpreted as requiring that the government compensate property owners for property taken to build highways, airports, or anything else that serves the public good.[13] But what if title to the property remains in the hands of the private property owner but the market value of the property diminishes because of laws that have been enacted or regulations the government has issued? Does this diminished value also constitute a taking for which the property owner is entitled to compensation? If a determination of critical habitat made by the Fish and Wildlife Service limits what a property owner can do with his or her property and if, as a result, the market value of the property decreases, is the property owner entitled to compensation?

That was the issue at stake in *Good v. United States,* a case filed with the United States Court of Federal Claims in 1997. Lloyd A. Good Jr.—the owner of a forty-acre tract of land in the Florida Keys, where he planned to develop a fifty-four-lot subdivision with a forty-eight-slip marina—alleged that the U.S. Army Corps of Engineers' refusal to grant him a permit to dredge and fill wetlands constituted a taking under the Fifth Amendment and entitled him to $2.5 million in compensation. Because the property provides a habitat for the Lower Keys marsh rabbit and the silver rice rat, which are listed as endangered species, the Fish and Wildlife Service had recommended that the corps not grant the permit.[14]

The claims court ruled that no taking had occurred. Judge James F. Merow, who delivered the opinion of the court, noted that land development is "a highly regulated business, and plaintiff's sought uses for his property were subject to restriction or prohibition under this regulatory regime." Merow concluded, "While plaintiff was free to assume the investment risks involved after considering that regime, the Fifth Amendment does not require the federal government to act as his surety should that investment prove to be ill-taken."[15]

TOWARD AN ENVIRONMENTAL ETHIC

I leave to legal scholars the question of whether the U.S. Supreme Court has correctly interpreted the Fifth Amendment and the Endangered

Species Act. What I am interested in here are the underlying philosophical issues—in particular, the question of whether there are moral and philosophical grounds for regulatory intervention to protect endangered species in situations in which it limits what private property owners can do with their property.

In a book published more than two decades ago, Ian G. Barbour maps out a far-ranging continuum of contrasting views about the relationship between humankind and nature. At one end of the spectrum, which Barbour labels the "unity with nature" school of thought, are those who view humankind as part of a larger whole, a view that emphasizes continuity with nature. At the other end of the spectrum, which Barbour labels the "domination over nature" school of thought, are those who believe that nature is there for people to exploit and do with as they see fit. Somewhere along the middle of the spectrum is the "stewardship of nature" school of thought, which holds that we ought to take good care of that with which we have been entrusted.[16]

There are insights to be gained from all three schools of thought. As those who have experienced the exhilarating joys of backpacking or canoeing in remote wilderness areas can attest, there is something wonderfully marvelous about nature. The psalmist captured a sense of this vastness and wonder centuries ago when exulting:

O Lord . . . how majestic is your name in all the earth!
You have set your glory above the heavens. . . .
When I look at your heavens, the work of your fingers,
the moon and the stars that you have established,
what are human beings that you are mindful of them,
mortals that you care for them? (Psalm 8.1, 3–4 NRSV)

The heavens above are not all that bring wonder and peace to our souls. As Henry David Thoreau put it in *Walden Pond*, "Heaven is under our feet as well as over our heads."[17] As Thoreau knew so well, each season brings its own set of joys when we allow ourselves to be immersed in nature. The music of trickling streams from melting snow as lush green new blades of grass poke through the reawakening ground that has shed its winter coat. The cool of a summer evening providing respite from the heat of day as fireflies punctuate the darkness with pinpoint bursts of light. The brilliantly clad scarlet maple trees of autumn, their bright red leaves contrasting sharply with the still-green grass, a powerful display of complementary colors one doesn't have to be an artist to appreciate. The late afternoon winter sun casting pastel blue shadows on fields blanketed with snow, the patches of sky near the horizon touched lightly with bluish green, the color of a robin's egg.

And sharing with us this wonderful world are creatures both large and small. Migrating warblers of many colors add their music to the melodious orchestra of the natural world as they flit about trees just beginning to leaf out. Black-masked raccoons quietly look for their next meal as a full moon bathes the landscape in soft, soothing light. V-shaped formations of Canada geese, honking in a language only they understand, head south as the crisp days of autumn signal the coming of winter. Bald eagles with their immense seven-foot wing spans quietly soar above open water in the cold of winter, their keen eyes on the lookout for fish that have injudiciously strayed too close to the surface.

In 1802 on a beach near Calais, France, William Wordsworth penned the following lines:

It is a beauteous evening, calm and free,
The holy time is quiet as a Nun
Breathless with adoration; the broad sun
Is sinking down in its tranquility;
The gentleness of heaven broods o'er the Sea.[18]

The wonder and grandeur of nature bring peace to our souls, stilling the tempests that rage within us. There is an intrinsic goodness to nature, goodness that we can experience if only, and only if, we pause to look at that which surrounds us and drink in the beauty of that which God has created—intrinsic goodness that registers on our consciousness only if we understand the importance of being still and opening our eyes and ears to that which surrounds us.[19]

Preserving trees and birds and other creatures that populate planet Earth is far more than just preserving other species, for to preserve the nature of which we are a part is to preserve wellsprings of renewal that refresh and nurture the human spirit, bringing greater depth and meaning to human existence.[20] Thoreau observed,

> We can never have enough of nature. We must be refreshed by the sight of inexhaustible vigor, vast and titanic in its features, the sea-coast with its wrecks, the wilderness with its living and decaying trees, the thundercloud, and the rain which lasts three weeks and produces freshets. We need to witness our limits transgressed, and some life pasturing freely where we never wander.[21]

DOMINATION OVER NATURE

At first glance, the opposite end of the spectrum—that of domination over nature—might appear to be at odds with the view that there is an intrinsic goodness to nature and that nature ought to be treasured and preserved. And, in part, it is. Susan Sontag observes, "Nature in America has always been suspect, on the defensive, cannibalized by progress."[22] Barbour says of the American experience,

> As the pioneers moved progressively westward, much that they encountered was hostile, a threat to survival, an obstacle to be overcome. Forests were cleared and wilderness destroyed to make way for civilization. . . . If timber was used up in one area, it could always be found somewhere else. Nature was treated as a source of raw materials in inexhaustible

quantities. Air, water, and land appeared ample to absorb the waste products of a burgeoning civilization.[23]

All of this might appear to suggest that there is nothing to recommend the domination-over-nature school of thought. That conclusion, however, is premature. There is a tendency on the part of those strongly committed to environmental protection to view the domination-over-nature school, with its strong emphasis on private property rights, as selfish, self-centered individuals hell-bent on squeezing every penny of profit from the land, even if this means destroying the land and the species that inhabit it, including *Homo sapiens*. To be sure, this is sometimes the case. But to paint all property-rights advocates with such unflattering colors is to perpetrate a gross injustice. As with the unity-with-nature perspective, the domination-over-nature perspective, with its strong emphasis on private property rights, gives expression to important insights about human existence and life as we know it.

It is worth noting that the psalmist who speaks of the majesty of God as reflected in the wonders of the heavens goes on to talk about God's having given human beings dominion over other creatures:

> You have given [human beings] dominion over the works of your hands;
> you have put all things under their feet,
> all sheep and oxen,
> and also the beasts of the field,
> the birds of the air, and the fish of the sea. (Psalm 8.6–8 NRSV)

To some it might seem odd that the psalmist goes from talking about how insignificant human beings are to describing them as having dominion over other creatures. Perhaps this is an odd juxtaposition. Yet there is something of profound significance at work here. As human beings, we are simultaneously insignificant parts of a greater whole and persons of significance in our own right. Nature is intrinsically valuable on its own merits; it far exceeds who we are and what we are capable of doing. At the same time, within certain limits, we assume power over it; it is valuable because it has value to us. This duality and the inherent tension that permeates it provide useful reference points for constructing an environmental ethic.

STEWARDSHIP OF NATURE

We now arrive at the third of the three perspectives on nature—stewardship of nature—found somewhere along the middle of the spectrum. This view holds that the natural world is something of great value that has been entrusted to us; we must care for and preserve it, as well as use it responsibly.

The Leopold Center for Sustainable Agriculture at Iowa State University is dedicated to encouraging and helping farmers practice sustainable agriculture, which Dennis R. Keeney, who served as director of the Leopold Center for a number of years, defines as "agricultural systems that are environmentally sound, profitable, and productive and that maintain the social fabric of the rural community."[24] Sally Puttmann, a family farmer in Iowa who has served on the Leopold Center's board of directors, sees sustainable agriculture as being supportive of farming practices "that will not only economically sustain the family that farms the land, but that will enhance the land long after my family is gone."[25]

The sustainable agriculture movement encourages farmers to till the soil and care for their crops and livestock in ways that are harmonious with the natural life processes rather than in ways that erode the topsoil, contaminate groundwater with dangerous chemicals, and otherwise harm ecosystems. At the same time, the sustainable agriculture movement gives recognition to the hopes, dreams, and economic needs of those who own the land and till the soil. It encourages stewardship in the most basic sense of the term.

PROPERTY RIGHTS, RESPECT FOR
OTHER PEOPLE, AND FREEDOM

I am content to leave to others the question of whether property rights exist in nature, as the seventeenth-century British philosopher John Locke suggested,[26] or whether they are mere social conventions. What I do wish to note is that in contemporary American society, property rights, as enshrined in constitutional guarantees and supported by centuries of Western law, are of tremendous significance.

Why are they so important? One reason is that respecting property rights is a way of respecting other people. While the Ten Commandments do not explicitly use the language of property rights, the notion is certainly implicit in the prohibition of killing, stealing, and coveting that which belongs to one's neighbor. In short, the Ten Commandments call upon us to respect our neighbor's life, family, and property, all of which are ways of showing respect for our neighbor. So property rights are, at least in part, about respecting other people—an important value in contemporary American society, a value many of us believe ought to be encouraged and promoted.

Property rights are also about freedom. One of the most exhilarating experiences that anyone can have is becoming a homeowner for the first time—having a place that is yours to do with as you see fit, a place that can be painted, wallpapered, and remodeled in whatever way pleases you. To be a property owner is to experience freedom, at least as long as our property doesn't end up owning us or causing us more trouble than it is worth.[27] (Our homes might be our castles, but a castle's not so great if we have to keep fixing the leaky roof and if the tax bill bankrupts us.)

The vigorous defenders of liberty who framed the U.S. Constitution placed strong emphasis on the protection of property rights—protection that was made more explicit in the Bill of Rights.[28] James Madison, an architect of both the Constitution and the Bill of Rights, commented, "Government is instituted to protect property of every sort,"[29]

an observation reminiscent of Locke's view that "the great and chief end
. . . of men's uniting into commonwealths and putting themselves under government is the preservation of their property."[30] In short, the
framers of the U.S. Constitution saw protection of property rights as essential if we are to experience liberty. By the same token, violations of
property rights came to be viewed as violations of liberty.

STEWARDSHIP AND FREEDOM WITHIN LIMITS

So property rights in society as we know it constitute a very special
form of liberty, a form of liberty protected by constitutional guarantees.
Yet it is not unlimited liberty. We might have the right to burn off the
grass and brush on land that we own but only if so doing does not
threaten our neighbors' homes or otherwise cause problems for them.[31]
We might have the right to plant anything we want on land that we
own but only if whatever we plant does not pose a significant risk to
our neighbors' crops or otherwise threaten their well-being.[32] In short,
the liberty that derives from property rights is not freedom without
limits. It is freedom within limits.

The notion of freedom within limits is intrinsic to the notion of
stewardship. Farmers who take the notion of stewardship seriously, as
given expression in the sustainable agriculture movement, still have a
range of property rights. They can decide which crops to plant and how
many acres to devote to each crop. They can decide which trees to cut
down and which to leave standing, which ponds to excavate and which
ponds to drain. They can decide where on their land to build new
houses and other buildings and what color to paint them. They can do
all of these things and much more—as long as they do not act in ways
at odds with the standards for environmental responsibility given expression in the sustainable agriculture movement (and, in some cases,
mandated by state or federal law).

And what about threatened and endangered species? While property owners have certain rights and a range of liberty, a faith that affirms that what God has created is good and hence of intrinsic value places limits on this freedom. We are not free to act in ways that are injurious to threatened and endangered species if our faith affirmations insist on the intrinsic goodness of all that God has created.

There are also other reasons for protecting threatened and endangered species. Other species contribute to human well-being, not simply because we derive pleasure from viewing eagles, condors, and peregrine falcons, but in many other ways as well.[33] In a book on biodiversity, Bonnie B. Burgess notes that benefits to humankind provided by other species include "natural medicines and the prototypes for synthetic pharmaceuticals, natural flood and pollution control, natural soil fertilization and pest control, climate control, the breakdown of waste material into elemental nutrients that are recycled for plant consumption, and the absorption of pollutants such as carbon dioxide."[34] In a letter sent to state representative Jack Metcalf (R-Wash.) a decade ago, ten physicians stated, "As medical professionals, we strongly believe the Endangered Species Act (ESA) protects not only endangered species but human health as well. Nearly one-quarter of prescription drugs distributed annually in the U.S. are based on substances derived from plants and animals."[35]

In short, when all things are considered, there is much to be said for protecting endangered and threatened species, thereby preserving biodiversity.

COMPETING PRIMA FACIE OBLIGATIONS

Now on to the hard issues. If people act in ways detrimental to threatened and endangered species, is intervention in order, be it in the form of the regulatory intervention authorized by the Endangered Species Act or in some other way? As noted throughout this volume, while intervention might sometimes be justifiable, it is something that ought to be done with great reluctance and only as a last resort. It must also be done only if the benefits to be gained from intervention are sufficient to offset the costs that invariably accompany intervention—in this case, costs to private property owners, measured in terms of their liberty and in economic terms. To put this in slightly different terms, it is plausible to argue that we have an obligation to be concerned not only about threatened and endangered species but also about the rights, autonomy, and well-being of private property owners. In short, as in so many other situations, there are competing prima facie obligations—in this case, prima facie obligations to take action to protect and preserve endangered and threatened species and prima facie obligations to respect the rights and autonomy of private property owners.

When confronted with competing prima facie obligations, the first thing that we typically do, be it in cases of this sort or in other situations, is to attempt to eliminate the conflict. Sometimes this can be done. For example, financial incentives for property owners who preserve and maintain critical habitat on their land might protect threatened and endangered species without regulatory intervention. James V. DeLong, an ardent defender of property rights, argues, "What if the government paid a bounty for every [threatened or endangered] species found on your land? Owners would compete to make their property attractive so as to lure species."[36]

Tax incentives could also be used to encourage preservation of critical habitat. One way of doing this would be to reduce real estate tax rates for landowners willing to make a long-term commitment to protecting and maintaining critical habitat. Another approach would be for the federal or state governments to allow these property owners tax credits that could be used toward federal or state income taxes.

There are, of course, some practical issues that need to be addressed. Since property tax revenues, which are typically collected by county governments, are the major source of funding for schools and vital municipal services, any reductions in tax rates for private property owners who preserve critical habitat for threatened or endangered species would have to be offset by revenue from other sources.

If revenue losses from environmentally based tax breaks were to be covered by federal or state subsidies, the question of where those monies would come from would have to be addressed—no easy matter in an era of massive federal budget deficits and at a time when many states are in difficult fiscal straits.[37] The same is true for allowing state or federal tax credits for habitat preservation and for offering property owners bonuses for providing habitat for threatened or endangered species.

These are difficult matters. But coming to grips with these basic realities is surely preferable to "liberalism on the cheap," whereby the government mandates that certain actions be taken but leaves it up to others to pick up the tab for doing so (an approach that generated considerable controversy in the 1980s and 1990s, when the federal government required that asbestos be removed from schools and other public buildings but did not fund the costly removal process).[38]

At the same time, wisdom is on the side of not being naively optimistic about prospects for encouraging voluntary compliance. Environmental preservation is not a vision that is universally shared. And any discussion of tax increases, even if for worthy purposes, evokes firestorms of controversy. It is easy to talk about financial incentives and other measures that would encourage property owners to preserve critical habitat; enacting, funding, and implementing these measures are quite different matters.

BUT IF NOT BY VOLUNTARY COMPLIANCE, THEN WHAT?

If efforts to encourage voluntary compliance fail, then what? At this point in the discussion, the ethics of intervention must be addressed. In the introduction, I suggested that the traditional just war criteria—just cause, right intent, last resort, lawful authority, reasonable hope of success, and due proportionality—provide useful guidelines for questions of intervention, including questions related to the Endangered Species Act. Two of the criteria—right intent and lawful authority—can be dealt with quite briefly. There is no reason to doubt that defenders of the Endangered Species Act have anything other than the best of intentions when advocating regulatory intervention to protect threatened and endangered species. And since the Endangered Species Act has withstood the test of constitutional review, the matter of lawful authority has been resolved to the satisfaction of all but the most diehard critics of the act. The other criteria, however, merit more detailed comment.

Just Cause?

On one level, the question of just cause can be quite simply answered: if that which God has created is good, shouldn't we protect threatened and endangered species? At first glance, this might appear to be a compelling argument—and in a sense it is. But as is so often the case, simple answers are frequently incomplete answers. Intervening to protect threatened and endangered species would without hesitation be an appropriate course of action were it not that something else is at stake in many of these situations, the something else being the rights and well-being of private property owners. And so the question becomes, To what extent is it morally justifiable to interfere with the liberty of private property owners and impose costs on them in an effort to protect and preserve threatened and endangered species? That's where matters start becoming more complicated. It is at this point that other criteria—in particular, last resort, reasonable hope of success, and due proportionality—come into play.

Last Resort?

As noted, there are alternatives to regulatory intervention—alternatives such as providing financial incentives to encourage property owners to protect and maintain critical habitat. But what if the political will, which in a democratic society derives its strength from the sentiments of the body politic, is not there to enact, fund, and implement such measures? In such situations, does regulatory intervention by default become the last resort?

It all depends. In particular, it depends on whether efforts are made to persuade the electorate to be supportive of special taxes or other measures that would make financial incentives possible. If such efforts are made but fail, regulatory intervention does indeed become the last resort, just as military action becomes the last resort when diplomacy and other nonmilitary attempts to resolve international disputes fail. In short, regulatory intervention to protect and preserve threatened and endangered species can be a last resort—but only after other options have been exhausted. Unfortunately, the political mind-set of the last half-century has often been to opt for regulatory intervention without exploring other options. Those in positions of responsibility have often been too quick to intervene and too slow to seek other solutions.

Reasonable Hope of Success?

There is no question that significant progress has been made in protecting and preserving certain threatened and endangered species. In fact, the numbers for some threatened and endangered species are increasing quite significantly. Examples include the following:

- In 1963, the bald eagle population in the lower forty-eight states had declined to just 417 known breeding pairs. Today there are nearly 8,000 pairs.[39] In 1999, the Clinton administration moved the bald eagle from the endangered species list to the threatened species list.[40] With the numbers continuing to increase, the Bush administration has announced plans to remove the bald eagle from the threatened species list, though bald eagles will still be protected by the federal Bald Eagle Protection Act of 1940.[41]

- In the early 1970s, the American peregrine falcon, one of nature's swiftest and most beautiful birds (they can dive at speeds of up to two hundred miles per hour to strike their prey), was on the brink of extinction. It had disappeared entirely from the eastern United States, with the numbers declining substantially in the western part of the country as well. As a result, it was among the first species to be listed as endangered under the provisions of the Endangered Species Act. It is no longer listed. The recovery of the American peregrine falcon—one of the greatest success stories of the environmental movement—enabled the U.S. Fish and Wildlife Service to remove the species from the list of endangered and threatened species on August 25, 1999.[42]

- Three decades ago, gray wolves were nearly extinct in the lower forty-eight states. Today, the number of gray wolves in Minnesota, Michigan, and Wisconsin has increased beyond the goals specified in the U.S. Fish and Wildlife Service species recovery plan. Since the three states have management plans in place to ensure the species' long-term survival, interior secretary Gale Norton has announced a proposal to remove gray wolves from the threatened species lists in those three states. "Thirty years ago, the future of the gray wolf in the United States outside of Alaska was anything but certain," she stated. "Today we celebrate not only the remarkable comeback of the gray wolf, but the partnerships, dedicated efforts and spirit of conservation that have made this success story possible."[43]

- In 1982, only twenty-four California condors were known to exist—three in captivity and twenty-one in the wild. Today, as the result of captive breeding programs and the release of young birds to their natural habitat, the number has more than tripled to seventy-five—sixty-six in captivity and nine in the wild.[44]

Examples such as these might be construed as suggesting that the Endangered Species Act is a resounding success. The situation, however, is far more complicated, defying simple analysis. For example, is the remarkable recovery of the bald eagle and the American peregrine falcon the result of the ban on DDT, a potent insecticide that adversely affected the reproduction rates of many species? The protection of critical habitat mandated by the Endangered Species Act? Or a combination of factors? A plausible argument can be made for the multifactor explanation, though that in no way diminishes the significance of the Endangered Species Act.[45]

Notwithstanding the success stories noted here, has the Endangered Species Act been all that effective? Critics suggest that it has not. In a stinging assessment issued by the Center for Biological Diversity, Kieran Suckling, Rhiwena Slack, and Brian Nowicki assert, "If extinction is the ultimate criteria by which to judge agency implementation of the ESA, the failure has been spectacular." They report that 114 species in the United States and U.S.-governed territories "are known to have become extinct in the first 20 years following the creation of the Endangered Species Act."[46]

Other critics suggest that, at least in part, the Endangered Species Act has been counterproductive by encouraging private property owners to get rid of critical habitat and endangered species on their land to avoid government-imposed restrictions on the use of their land. Michael L. Rosenzweig, who teaches ecology and evolutionary biology at the University of Arizona, observes, "The Endangered Species Act's relationship to the private landowner is altogether pernicious. Whoever ruins the land for wild creatures goes unscathed and continues to have the unrestricted right to exploit it. Meanwhile, whoever improves the world for a rare species gets punished [by being subjected to restrictions]."[47]

In a report entitled *Rebuilding the Ark: Toward a More Effective Endangered Species Act for Private Land,* David S. Wilcove, Michael J. Bean, Robert Bonnie, and Margaret McMillan acknowledge that this paradox is a problem:

> Many landowners are capable of helping endangered species by creating, restoring, or enhancing habitat on their land, but are unwilling to do so. Their unwillingness often stems from fear of new restrictions. They are afraid that if they take actions that attract new endangered species to their land or increase the populations of the endangered species that are already there, their "reward" for doing so will be more regulatory restrictions on the use of their property. In its most extreme manifestation, this fear has prompted some landowners to destroy unoccupied habitats of endangered species before the animals could find it. One landowner, referring to the presence of red-cockaded woodpeckers on a small section of his property, announced, "I cannot afford to let those woodpeckers take over the rest of my property. I'm going to start massive clearcutting."[48]

When all things are considered, the efficacy of the Endangered Species Act is difficult to assess. However, as the examples illustrate, it is plausible to argue that the act has had at least some impact on the preservation of threatened and endangered species, and it is reasonable to assume that it will continue to do so in the years to come.

Proportionality?

The even more difficult question is whether the costs associated with implementation of the Endangered Species Act are sufficient to offset whatever benefits derive from the act. In part, this is a difficult matter to assess because the costs related to the act are hard to isolate. The Center for Biological Diversity estimates that providing full funding for the listing process and the designation of critical habitat would add up to $31 million per year,[49] a relatively modest amount in the overall scheme of things. That, however, represents only a small portion of the costs associated with the act. A more complete list of the costs would include

- the cost of litigation related to the act (the costs incurred by various levels of government and the costs incurred by groups and individuals initiating legal action);

- the cost of establishing and maintaining critical habitat plans;

- the cost to private property owners when critical habitat designations diminish the market value of their property; and

- the cost to potential home buyers when restrictions on logging old-growth forests and other restrictions increase the cost of lumber (as a result of logging being shifted to more expensive areas) and in turn the market price of homes.

It might be added that these are just the economic costs. Other costs include emotional costs—for example, the anger that results from what is perceived as excessive and inappropriate government intervention—and the cost to other projects when time and money are spent on controversies related to the Endangered Species Act.

What is the bottom line in all of this? It is possible—perhaps even probable—that the benefits of the Endangered Species Act are sufficient to offset the substantial costs related to the act. A far stronger case can be made, however, for reforming the act to maximize benefits while reducing the costs associated with it.

SOME REFORMS WORTHY OF CONSIDERATION

Before mapping out some possible reforms worthy of consideration, it should be noted that some changes in the regulatory intervention authorized by the Endangered Species Act have been made in an effort to decrease the conflict between the provisions of the act and private property rights. One of the most significant of these is the "safe harbor" policy, which assures landowners who agree to take measures to protect critical habitat that they will not be subjected to additional property-use restrictions during the period of time specified in the agreement.[50]

The safe harbor policy is a step in the right direction. But more needs to be done. Reforms worthy of consideration include the following:

- *Change federal estate tax law (inheritance tax law) to allow reduced rates for land that is part of a long-term critical habitat plan.*[51] In *Rebuilding the Ark*, the authors propose, "In cases where the property could be managed to benefit endangered species, the heirs should be given the opportunity to defer part of the estate taxes by entering into a management agreement with the Department of the Interior."[52] That's an approach worth exploring.

- *Modify the safe harbor policy to provide financial incentives for private landowners.* Currently, the only reward landowners get for entering into a safe harbor agreement are promises that they will not be hit with additional restrictions and that when the contractual period has expired, they have the right to undo whatever steps they took to create and protect critical habitat. The pot could be sweetened by making reduced federal estate tax provisions automatically applicable to land covered by a safe harbor agreement, provided the heirs continue the agreement.[53]

- *Exempt from the provisions of the Endangered Species Act small parcels of privately owned land that are not part of larger ecosystems critical for the survival of threatened and endangered species.* Fragmented parcels of land do little, if anything, to help ensure the survival of many threatened and endangered species. When such is the case, regulatory intervention imposes significant costs on landowners without sufficient benefit to offset these costs. If little, if anything, is to be gained by regulatory intervention, why provoke unnecessary controversy?

- *Establish priorities among threatened and endangered species with respect to preservation.* Currently, the Endangered Species Act requires that efforts be made to protect all threatened and endangered species. While this is laudable on a theoretical level, on a practical level it is shortsighted because resources are stretched so thin that, ironically, many threatened and endangered species perish because of delays in the listing process or because of inadequate efforts to secure critical habitat for them. And how should priorities be established? On the basis of two factors: public support for preservation; and potential benefit, such as being a source of crucial ingredients for lifesaving medicines. Public support is important, both in terms of securing adequate funding for preservation programs and in terms of softening controversies related to conflicts with private property rights. Put in slightly different words, it is much easier to sell the public (and private property owners) on measures to protect and preserve the bald eagle than it is to sell the public (and private property owners) on measures to preserve the Kanab ambersnail (unless, of course, there were reason to believe that the Kanab ambersnail might be a source of a type of medicine useful in treating a deadly disease such as cancer). And what if there is not a discernible public preference for one species over another? In a book on the Endangered Species Act, Brian Czech and Paul R. Krausman propose the following prioritization (going from most important to least important): birds and mammals, fish, plants, reptiles, amphibians, invertebrates, and microorganisms.[54] Their priority list has considerable merit.

SOME CONCLUDING CONSIDERATIONS

One-dimensional approaches to controversial matters such as the Endangered Species Act are almost always the easiest courses of action to take. Environmentalists who are single-minded in their pursuit of environmental objectives and private property advocates who focus on nothing other than private property rights never have difficulty determining where they stand. Being multidimensional—being concerned about environmental preservation and private property rights—is far more challenging.

Yet the simple is not always the preferable. Indeed, there is much to be said for multidimensional approaches that take into account a variety of considerations. In the introduction, it was noted that just war theory is the middle ground between the crusading approach to war and pacifism. Both the crusading approach and pacifism are one-dimensional, with zealots of vastly different persuasions in both camps. But zeal does not equate with wisdom. Just war theory has always struck me as possessing greater wisdom than either extreme: it is a multidimensional approach suggesting that war is not always justified but that when it is justified, it is at best the lesser of evils. The same is true of multidimensional approaches to questions of intervention related to the Endangered Species Act and all of the other complex and difficult issues addressed in this volume.

NOTES

1. Michael J. Bean, "Endangered Species: Endangered Act?" *Environment* (January 1999), at www.findarticles.com/cf_dls/m1076/1_41/53709851/pl/ article.jhtml (accessed April 11, 2003). The Environmental Defense Fund has been renamed Environmental Defense. Its website can be accessed at www.edf .org. Other environmental groups and organizations supportive of the Endangered Species Act include the Sierra Club (www.sierraclub.org), the National

Wildlife Federation (www.nwf.org), Defenders of Wildlife (www.defenders .org), the National Resources Defense Council (www.nrdc.org), and Earthjustice (www.earthjustice.org).

2. The National Endangered Species Act Reform Coalition, "How Has the ESA Impacted America?" at www.nesarc.org/stories.htm (accessed March 12, 2004). The summary is based on an editorial entitled "A Snail Retreat," which ran in the *Wall Street Journal,* December 27, 1993. The National Endangered Species Act Reform Coalition (www.nesarc.org) is a coalition of more than a hundred organizations, among them the American Farm Bureau Federation, the National Association of Home Builders, and the National Rural Electric Cooperative Association. Other groups and organizations supportive of private property rights and critical of the Endangered Species Act include the Competitive Enterprise Institute (www.cei.org), Defenders of Property Rights (www.defendersproprights.org), the Center for the Defense of True Enterprise (www.propertyrightsresearch.org), and the League of Private Property Voters (www.landrights.org).

3. The Endangered Species Preservation Act of 1966 and the Endangered Species Conservation Act of 1969 helped set the stage for the Endangered Species Act of 1973. A 1973 conference held in Washington, D.C., resulted in the Convention on International Trade in Endangered Species of Wild Fauna and Flora (CITES), which restricted international commerce in plant and animal species believed to be threatened. The Endangered Species Act of 1973, passed later that year, combined and substantially strengthened the provisions of previous legislation while also breaking new ground (U.S. Fish and Wildlife Service, "History and Evolution of the Endangered Species Act of 1973, Including Its Relationship to CITES," at http://endangered.fws.gov/esasum .html (accessed March 12, 2004).

4. When the U.S. House of Representatives originally voted on the bill, the vote was 390–12 in favor. When the final vote was taken after the bill came out of conference committee, the vote was 355–4 in favor. The original vote in the Senate was 99–1 in favor, with the bill gaining approval without dissent after it came out of conference committee (*Congressional Record* 119, part 33 [December 19 and 20, 1973], 42528–35, 42910, 42915–16).

5. Quoted by Bonnie B. Burgess in *Fate of the Wild: The Endangered Species Act and the Future of Biodiversity* (Athens: University of Georgia Press, 2001), 3. The signing of the act, it might be added, did not make much of a ripple. The *New York Times,* for example, buried the signing of the bill as a

brief addendum to a story about another bill the president signed the same day ("President Signs Manpower Bill: States and Communities Get Larger Role in Job and Training Programs," *New York Times*, December 28, 1973, 1, 13).

6. U.S. Fish and Wildlife Service, "History and Evolution."

7. Endangered Species Act of 1973, sec. 3 (5) (6) (19), at http://endangered .fws.gov/esa.html (accessed March 12, 2004). And what constitutes a species? The act states, "The term 'species' includes any subspecies of fish or wildlife or plants, and any distinct population segment of any species of vertebrate fish or wildlife which interbreeds when mature," sec. 3 (15). Note: Sec. 3 (11) of the original measure was subsequently repealed, resulting in paragraphs 12–21 being renumbered as paragraphs 11–20.

8. Endangered Species Act of 1973, sec. 4 (1) (3).

9. Burgess, *Fate of the Wild*, 10–11.

10. Supreme Court of the United States, *Tennessee Valley Authority v. Hill et al.*, 437 U.S. 153 (1978). The following year, however, Senator Howard Baker and Representative John Duncan Sr., both of Tennessee, added an amendment to the Energy and Water Development Appropriations Act exempting the Tellico project from the Endangered Species Act, legislation that became law when signed by President Jimmy Carter. Subsequently, several other populations of the snail darter were discovered, and it was listed as a threatened species rather than as an endangered species (Forest History Society, "1979 Snail Darter Exemption Case," at www.lib.duke.edu/forest/usfscoll/ policy/northern_spotted_owl/1979owl.snaildarter.html [accessed April 6, 2004]).

11. During this same period, the number of threatened and endangered species listed by the Fish and Wildlife Service increased substantially, which had the practical impact of increasing the number of cases in which intervention was a possibility.

12. Supreme Court of the United States, *Babbitt v. Sweet Home Chapter of Communities for a Great Oregon*, 515 U.S. 687 (1995).

13. The long-standing legal doctrine of eminent domain allows the government to condemn privately held property and force the individuals who own it to sell it to the government to be used for the construction of roads or other projects deemed beneficial to society. The Illinois State Office of the Attorney General defines eminent domain as follows: "Eminent domain is the sovereign right to acquire private property for public use. The right of eminent domain is held by each state and the federal government. State legislatures can

delegate the right to local governments, government-related agencies, public utilities and railroads" (Office of the Attorney General, State of Illinois, *Eminent Domain: A Guide to Understanding Your Rights under Law*, at www.ag.state .il.us/publications/eminent.htm [accessed October 5, 2001]). While there are some who believe that various levels of government are excessively eager in their use of this doctrine (see, e.g., Larry Salzman, "New Eminent Domain Assaults: Taking Private Property for Political Elite," at www.aynrand.org/ medialink/eminent.shtml [accessed October 5, 2001]), few, if any, would argue that the doctrine should be totally abandoned. Were it not for this long-standing doctrine, one recalcitrant individual could block the construction of a new highway or airport by refusing to sell the right-of-way needed for the project. At the same time, unrestrained use of the powers inherent in the doctrine flies in the face of cherished liberties. For a thoughtful discussion of the conflict between the individual and the state inherent in the doctrine of eminent domain, see Richard A. Epstein, *Takings: Private Property and the Power of Eminent Domain* (Cambridge, Mass.: Harvard University Press, 1985). Epstein states, "My thesis is that the eminent domain approach, as applied both to personal liberty and private property, offers a principled account of both the functions of the state and the limitations upon its powers" (331).

14. United States Court of Federal Claims, *Good v. United States*, 39 Fed.Cl. 81 (1997). Though in an earlier opinion the Fish and Wildlife Service had concluded that the proposed project would have no effect on the endangered rabbit, the agency, after further study, noted that the populations of the marsh rabbit and the silver rice rat were declining and concluded that development of the property would place the continued existence of these endangered species in jeopardy.

15. *Good v. United States* (1997). The courts have tended to make a distinction between regulatory intervention that totally (or almost totally) destroys the value of property and regulatory intervention that merely diminishes the value of property. Consider, for example, *Pennsylvania Coal v. Mahon* (260 U.S. 393 [1922]). H. J. Mahon had purchased a home on land where the Pennsylvania Coal Company had retained ownership of subsurface coal deposits. Subsequent to Mahon's purchase of the home, Pennsylvania passed a law prohibiting the mining of coal under residences, thereby preventing Pennsylvania Coal from mining the coal. The U.S. Supreme Court ruled that this regulatory intervention constituted a taking. Justice Oliver Wendell Holmes, who delivered the opinion of the Court, stated, "Government hardly could go

on if to some extent values incident to property could not be diminished without paying for every such change in the general law. . . . But obviously the implied limitation must have its limits. . . . One factor for consideration in determining such limits is the extent of the diminution. When it reaches a certain magnitude, in most if not in all cases there must be an exercise of eminent domain and compensation to sustain the act."

The U.S. Supreme Court issued a similar ruling in *Lucas v. South Carolina Coastal Council* (505 U.S. 1103 [1992]), more than a half-century later. In 1977, David H. Lucas purchased two lots on a barrier island that, at the time of purchase, was zoned for single-family residential construction. He paid $975,000 for the two lots. In 1986, however, South Carolina enacted a beachfront management act that prohibited construction of "occupable improvements" on the island. The Court determined that "the takings clause of the Federal Constitution's Fifth Amendment is violated when land-use regulation . . . denies an owner economically viable use of his or her land." A South Carolina court awarded Lucas $1,232,000 as compensation for the lost use of his lots (Bernard H. Siegan, *Property and Freedom: The Constitution, the Courts, and Land-Use Regulation* [New Brunswick, N.J.: Transaction Publishers, 1997], 128.

However, in *Miller v. Schoene* (276 U.S. 272 [1928]), the U.S. Supreme Court ruled that "the owner of ornamental cedar trees is not deprived of his property without due process of law by the state requiring the destruction of the trees to avoid the infecting of apple orchards in the vicinity with cedar rust." And in *Penn Central Transportation Co. v. New York City* (438 U.S. 104 [1978]), the U.S. Supreme Court ruled that New York City's landmarks preservation law, which limited what Penn Central could do with the airspace above Grand Central Terminal, "did not effect a 'taking' of private property by the government without just compensation in violation of the Fifth and Fourteenth Amendments, since (1) the law did not interfere with the present uses of the building . . . (2) the law did not necessarily prohibit occupancy of any of the air space above the landmark building, since under the procedures of the law, it was possible that some construction in the air space might be allowed, and (3) the law did not deny all use of the owner's preexisting air rights above the landmark building."

16. Ian G. Barbour, *Technology, Environment, and Human Values* (New York: Praeger Publishers, 1980), 13–34. I have changed the order in which Barbour lists these three schools of thought.

17. Henry David Thoreau, "The Pond in Winter," in *Walden Pond; or, Life in the Woods* (New York: New American Library, 1942), 189.

18. William Wordsworth, "It Is a Beauteous Evening, Calm and Free," in *The Complete Poetical Works of William Wordsworth*, Cambridge edition (Boston: Houghton Mifflin, 1904), 285.

19. The creation story found in Genesis 1 states, "And God said, 'Let the earth bring forth living creatures of every kind: cattle and creeping things and wild animals of the earth of every kind.' And it was so. God made the wild animals of the earth of every kind, and the cattle of every kind, and everything that creeps upon the ground of every kind. And God saw that it was good" (Gen. 1.24–25 NRSV).

20. There is room for debate about whether humankind is a part of nature or exists apart from nature. I am inclined toward the former.

21. Thoreau, "Spring," in *Walden Pond*, 211.

22. Susan Sontag, "Melancholy Objects," in *On Photography* (New York: Farrar, Straus and Giroux, 1977), 65.

23. Barbour, *Technology, Environment, and Human Values*, 16.

24. Dennis R. Keeney, "Toward a Sustainable Agriculture: Need for Clarification of Concepts and Terminology," *American Journal of Alternative Agriculture* 4, nos. 3–4 (1989): 102. Additional information about the Leopold Center for Sustainable Agriculture is available at the center's website: www.leopold.iastate.edu.

25. Quoted in *Leopold Letter: A Newsletter of the Leopold Center for Sustainable Agriculture* 7 (Summer 1995): 2.

26. In a widely quoted passage, John Locke asserts that "we must consider what state all men are naturally in, and that is a state of perfect freedom to order their actions and dispose of their possessions and persons as they see fit, within the bounds of the law of nature, without asking leave or depending upon the will of any other man" (*The Second Treatise of Government*, ed. Thomas P. Peardon [Indianapolis, Ind.: Bobbs-Merrill, 1952], 4, sec. 4).

27. In a poignant passage, Max Weber notes that the Puritan moralist Richard Baxter held that material goods should be "like a light cloak which can be thrown aside at any moment" but in industrialized society have "gained inexorable power over the lives of men" and have "become an iron cage" (*The Protestant Ethic and the Spirit of Capitalism*, tr. Talcott Parsons [New York: Charles Scribner's Sons, 1958], 181). And how do we become entrapped by our possessions? By digging ourselves in too deep financially. By never being

satisfied with what we have. By having more than we can take care of. Having property can be liberating. But so also can not having property.

28. The U.S. Constitution, as originally drafted and ratified, says relatively little about property rights. Alexander Hamilton argued that this really was not a problem, because the power of the federal government was limited to what the Constitution explicitly authorized it to do. Hamilton wrote, "For why declare that things shall not be done that there is no power to do? Why, for instance, should it be said that liberty of the press shall not be restrained, when no power is given by which restriction be imposed?" (Alexander Hamilton, "The Lack of a Bill of Rights," *Federalist No. 84*, in Alexander Hamilton, James Madison, and John Jay, *The Federalist*, ed. Benjamin Fletcher Wright [Cambridge, Mass.: Belknap Press / Harvard University Press, 1961], 531). However, those concerned about individual rights, including property rights, wanted a more explicit prohibition of encroachment on individual liberties. The result was the Bill of Rights, which, as Siegan notes, "shielded from federal intrusion those property interests of most concern during that period: one's home, land, office, firearms, and financial resources" (*Property and Freedom*, 20).

29. Quoted by Siegan in *Property and Freedom*, 14. The quotation is from an essay by James Madison that was published in the *National Gazette*, March 29, 1792.

30. Locke, *Second Treatise*, 71, sec. 124.

31. One of the greatest tragedies that has happened anywhere occurred in and around the small town of Peshtigo, Wisconsin, on October 8, 1871. The abnormally dry summer had provided settlers and loggers with an opportunity to burn brush and debris left from logging. But on the night of October 8, strong winds whipped up the fires that had been set, resulting in a huge conflagration that burned over a million acres of land, including virtually the entire town of Peshtigo. The loss of life was horrific. The death toll is believed to be somewhere in the vicinity of fifteen hundred lives—far greater than the loss of life in the great Chicago fire, which occurred the same day and, because it happened in a major city, received far more attention in the press than the Peshtigo fire (*Great Peshtigo Fire of 1871*, at www.idbsu.edu/history/ncasner/hy210/peshtigo.htm [accessed March 31, 2004]).

32. As noted, in *Miller v. Schoene* (276 U.S. 272 [1928]), the U.S. Supreme Court ruled that "the owner of ornamental cedar trees is not de-

prived of his property without due process of law by the state requiring the destruction of the trees to avoid the infecting of apple orchards in the vicinity with cedar rust."

33. A good deal of debate among environmental ethicists revolves around the question of whether environmental ethics should be anthropocentric (i.e., emphasize the significance of other species for human well-being) or should take into account the intrinsic value (some would say "rights") of other species. I see no inherent contradiction in combining both approaches.

34. Burgess, *Fate of the Wild*, 30.

35. Quoted by Burgess in *Fate of the Wild*, 55.

36. James V. DeLong, *Property Matters: How Property Rights Are under Assault—and Why You Should Care* (New York: Free Press, 1997), 105.

37. At a bare minimum, however, there is an argument to be made for saying that revenues derived from environmental fees ought to be used for environmental preservation. Consider, for example, what has transpired in Illinois. The state was facing a $5 billion budget deficit when Governor Rod Blagojevich took office in 2003. Having promised that he would not raise income or sales taxes, he had to look elsewhere for revenues. The elsewhere included raising environmental fees and transferring a significant portion of the new revenues generated to the general revenue fund, thus using revenue generated by environmental fees to finance other programs and activities. (The details are specified in Illinois Public Act 93-003, at www.legis.state.il.us/legislation/publicacts/fulltext .asp?Name=093–0032&print=true [accessed April 6, 2004]).

38. The unfunded mandate controversy resulted in the enactment of the Unfunded Mandates Reform Act of 1995, which requires that Congress and federal agencies consider cost to state, local, and tribal governments and to the private sector before imposing federal requirements that necessitate spending by these government units or by the private sector. (A summary of the act and other legislative measures can be found at http://ipl.unm.edu/cwl/fedbook/ unfunded.html [accessed April 12, 2004].)

39. *American Bald Eagle Information,* at www.baldeagleinfo.com (June 28, 2004).

40. "Bald Eagle Flies off Endangered List," *CNN.com*, July 2, 1999, at www.cnn.com/NATURE/9907/02/bald.eagle.02/index.html (accessed June 28, 2004).

41. *American Bald Eagle Information* (see n. 39).

42. U.S. Fish and Wildlife Service, *Endangered Species Program: American Peregrine Falcon,* at http://endangered.fws.gov/i/b/sab22.html (accessed July 26, 2004).

43. "Norton Announces Proposal to Remove Eastern Population of Gray Wolves from Endangered Species Act," U.S. Fish and Wildlife Service News Release, July 16, 2004, at http://mountain-prairie.fws.gov/pressrel/DC412 .htm (accessed July 21, 2004). The two other populations of gray wolves in the lower forty-eight states—the Rocky Mountain population in Idaho, Wyoming, and Montana and the Southwestern population of Mexican gray wolves—will continue to be listed, though progress is being made in these areas as well. For detailed information on the Rocky Mountain population, see U.S. Fish and Wildlife Service, Nez Perce Tribe, National Park Service, and U. S. Department of Agriculture, Wildlife Services, *Rocky Mountain Wolf Recovery 2003 Annual Report,* ed. T. Meier (Helena, Mont.: U.S. Fish and Wildlife Service, Ecological Services, 2004).

44. Oliver H. Pattee and Robert Mesta, "California Condors," at http:// biology.usgs.gov/s+t/noframe/b162.htm (accessed July 21, 2004).

45. The recovery of the American peregrine falcon was also helped by captive breeding programs that raised young falcons to be released.

46. Kieran Suckling, Rhiwena Slack, and Brian Nowicki, *Extinction and the Endangered Species Act* (Center for Biological Diversity, 2004), 2, available at www.biologicaldiversity.org/swcbd/Programs/policy/esa/eesa.html [accessed April 22, 2004]). The criticism that Suckling, Slack, and Nowicki make is directed more toward the implementation of the Endangered Species Act (or lack thereof), rather than toward the act itself. In particular, they argue that lengthy delays in listing threatened and endangered species have been detrimental to the survival of these species.

47. Michael L. Rosenzweig, as quoted by Malcolm G. Scully, "Protecting the Endangered Species Act," *Chronicle of Higher Education,* May 2, 2003.

48. David S. Wilcove, Michael J. Bean, Robert Bonnie, and Margaret McMillan, *Rebuilding the Ark: Toward a More Effective Endangered Species Act for Private Land,* at www.edf.org/documents/483_Rebuilding%20the%20Ark.htm (accessed July 26, 2004).

49. Suckling, Slack, and Nowicki, *Extinction and the Endangered Species Act,* 8.

50. See, for example, U.S. Fish and Wildlife Service, Robert Russell, and Oregon Fish and Wildlife Department, *Safe Harbor Agreement for the Oregon Chub,* at www.edf.org/documents/613_ORchubfulltext.pdf (accessed July 26,

2004), and *Safe Harbor Agreement with James W. Crosswhite for Voluntary Enhancement and Restoration Activities Benefitting the Southwestern Willow Flycatcher and the Little Colorado Spinedace in Nutrioso Creek, Arizona,* at http://arizonaes.fws.gov/Documents/Safe%20Harbors/SHA%208_29_03_FINAL.pdf (accessed July 26, 2004). The agreement with Russell covers a period of five years while that with Crosswhite is for fifty years. Michael J. Bean, who, as noted, is affiliated with the Environmental Defense Fund, is credited with proposing the safe harbor policy. For an overview of the provision, see Burgess, *Fate of the Wild,* 125–26.

51. The federal estate tax is being phased out over a period of several years, with the entire tax to be repealed in 2010. But because Congress could not reach consensus and instead passed a compromise bill, the estate tax is scheduled to revert to the 2001 level (55 percent) in 2011. No one expects Congress to allow that to happen without revisiting the issue. Many expect reform rather than repeal—that is, continuation of the federal estate tax but at a reduced level. When the issue is revisited, there will be an opportunity to include environmental incentives in a revised estate tax law. (The Cornell University Legal Information Institute website provides a useful overview of estate tax law, www.law.cornell.edu/topics/estate_gift_tax.html, that includes links to relevant sections of the U.S. code.)

52. Wilcove et al., *Rebuilding the Ark,* 8.

53. Compare Wilcove et al., *Rebuilding the Ark,* 8.

54. Brian Czech and Paul R. Krausman, *The Endangered Species Act: History, Conservation Biology, and Public Policy* (Baltimore: Johns Hopkins University Press, 2001), 71, 150–51.

Ten Questions for Reflection and Discussion

1 Why, if at all, should we protect threatened and endangered species?

2 Why, if at all, should property rights be respected?

3 When, if at all, is it appropriate to limit what landowners can do with their property?

4 To what extent, if at all, should landowners be compensated if environmental restrictions decrease the value of their property?

5 What changes, if any, should be made in the Endangered Species Act?

6 Should all species be preserved? Or are there some that should not be preserved—perhaps even destroyed?

7 Should priorities be established for the preservation of threatened and endangered species? And if so, what should these priorities be?

8 If financial incentives were to be offered to encourage landowners to preserve critical habitat, what form should these financial incentives take?

9 How should the cost of these incentives be covered?

10 What is your assessment of the unity-with-nature, domination-over-nature, and stewardship schools of thought? What are the strengths and weaknesses of each approach?

INDEX

—

ABOUT THE AUTHOR

—

Daniel E. Lee is professor of ethics at Augustana College (Illinois) and director of the Augustana Center for the Study of Ethics.